ANGLICAN
PUBLIC WORSHIP

# ANGLICAN PUBLIC WORSHIP

COLIN DUNLOP
*Dean of Lincoln*

WIPF & STOCK · Eugene, Oregon

DEDICATED
WITH AFFECTION AND RESPECT
TO
JAMES HERBERT SRAWLEY, D.D.

*Prebendary of Heydour cum Walton
in Lincoln Cathedral
Honorary Fellow of Selwyn College
Cambridge*

Wipf and Stock Publishers
199 W 8th Ave, Suite 3
Eugene, OR 97401

Anglican Public Worship
By Dunlop, Colin
Copyright©1961 SCM
ISBN 13: 978-1-62032-026-6
Publication date 1/11/2012
Previously published by SCM, 1961

Copyright © D.C Dunlop 1961

Revised edition 1961 by SCM Press.
This edition published by arrangement
with Hymns Ancient & Modern Ltd.

## CONTENTS

| | | |
|---|---|---|
| I | THE JUSTIFICATION OF PUBLIC WORSHIP | 7 |
| II | THE BACKGROUND OF PUBLIC WORSHIP | 19 |
| III | THE MATERIALS OF WORSHIP (1) Words | 29 |
| IV | THE MATERIALS OF WORSHIP (2) Music | 41 |
| V | THE MATERIALS OF WORSHIP (3) Ceremonial | 50 |
| VI | THE BOOK OF COMMON PRAYER | 61 |
| VII | EUCHARIST AND SACRIFICE | 77 |
| VIII | THE ORDER OF THE HOLY COMMUNION | 88 |
| IX | MORNING AND EVENING PRAYERS | 102 |
| X | PRAYER BOOK REVISION | 125 |
| | INDEX | 139 |

# ACKNOWLEDGEMENTS

My gratitude is due to Dr. Srawley and to my wife for reading through my MS. and making valuable criticisms and suggestions.

# I

# THE JUSTIFICATION OF PUBLIC WORSHIP

THE view has got round that worship is an optional element in true Christianity, and that a Christian character can exist more or less in its perfection in a man who never worships. From being a test of the true condition of a Christian soul, just and charitable conduct has come to be regarded as Christianity itself, complete and entire. Towards such conduct a habit of worship may or may not contribute, but, even at its highest estimation, it is purely a means to an end. More commonly its value even in this capacity is doubted, and 'going to church' is reckoned as a habit more or less irrelevant at its best, but possibly harmful in the long run. For public worship must lead to association with other churchgoers, who as a body are not supposed to be interested in 'the realities' of religion, but are notoriously preoccupied with 'the minutiae' of dogma and ecclesiastical propriety and are moreover uncharitable and backbiting in their mutual relations. All this cannot but be harmful to the man who wishes to be a real Christian, so he in the end has no choice but to dissociate himself from church membership with its characteristic activity of worship, and to plough a lonely furrow in his pursuit of moral perfection.

This is crudely put, and probably as a statement might not be made in its entirety by many thoughtful individuals. Yet it reflects broadly a common estimate of the spiritual status of public worship, namely a means to an end, though of doubtful value even as such.

It must be remembered also that social conditions to-day

are such as to tempt people rather powerfully to search for reasons and arguments against public worship. The sense of community even in small localities has long been weakening, and there is in consequence, a growing disinclination to assemble together for any purpose which cannot provide the individual with some obvious and immediate gain. Thus large crowds will assemble for concerts or racing, while trades union meetings or lectures by others than celebrities are notoriously neglected. In addition to this the possibilities for spending Sundays in pleasant ways not available in former times are increasing. Both these facts tempt people to find well-sounding excuses for abandoning public worship and it is not hard to do this. But the excuses when framed nearly always assume that the exclusive purpose of public worship is help to the individual in his private pursuit of moral perfection; in other words they assume worship to be a means to an end. If it can be shown that public worship does not deliver immediately and obviously, even to a casual attender, inspiration to aim higher in moral endeavour, then it can fairly be asserted that public worship has no place in the truly Christian scheme of things. As this is not very easy to demonstrate, the objector feels he has won his case and public worship is deemed to have forfeited its spiritual status.

The short-term view inherent in such a judgment will be noticed. As a matter of fact a long-practised habit of worship does set its seal upon the worshipper: he does become a man with a readier response to moral demands, a quickened sense of ethical responsibility. But contemporary man in general is unaccustomed to consider long-term views. The principle of cash-on-delivery possesses his imagination: the quick results of mechanized processes have speeded up the tempo of life and keyed up human expectations. Only what happens rapidly is noticed: the seed growing secretly is written off as a failure: long before it shoots up, the attention has impatiently strayed to fresh ground. So the long-term results of public worship are not observed: the sole material for

## THE JUSTIFICATION OF PUBLIC WORSHIP 9

judgment is 'When I come out of church I don't feel any better'.

These then are some of the reasons for the low opinion of the value of public worship commonly held. And this opinion has put the believer in public worship on the defensive. As it appears no longer of much use to urge the *duty* of worship, it has become customary to plead the *benefits* of worship. But the mistake is often made of defending public worship on the same level from which it is attacked and of accepting the premises of the objector. Thus it is sometimes urged, and quite truly urged, that to enter church upon a Sunday is tantamount to 'giving your vote for God' in a world where God is widely ignored. But the objector will reply that a far more fruitful vote for God is to clothe the naked or feed the hungry or relieve the oppressed either by direct action or by indirect political activity; he may add that the need for this kind of witness is actually obscured in the habit of churchgoing, even quoting from the Prophets to reinforce his charge. The defender of public worship will have a difficult time of it. He has joined issue in defending a by-product of worship, rather than by leading the critic to the heart of the matter.

Similarly a man will seek to raise the status of public worship by affirming that the worshipper takes his place in the fellowship of the Church; that to let his place be empty is to weaken the corporate effort of all believers. To which the critic will reply that the corporate effort of the Church might be better diverted from hymns and psalms to a collective discussion as to how the principles of the Sermon on the Mount might be applied to the life of the neighbourhood. Here again the mistake is made of not going to the root of the matter and of allowing the critic to go on assuming that the Church is primarily a society for improving the economic conditions of human life.

But church services, it is sometimes urged, are valuable because they provide an inspiration for Christian living during the six days ahead. That may indeed often be true, but only if the worshipper is not primarily seeking that inspiration, and is engaged upon some less self-regarding activity. If you go to church deliberately seeking edification and moral inspiration above all things, the chances are not in favour of success. And if we advocate public worship for its capacity to inspire good works, we are once more diverting men's minds from its true nature and aim; we are attracting attention to one long-term result which will only follow if the main motive is something different.

For the fact is that whenever worship is thought of as essentially a means to some human end, however lofty, its pursuit will surely be disappointing. Such an estimate is bound up with an ultimate belief that God exists for man and heaven for earth, and that nothing is of value unless it can be shown to contribute a more or less immediate benefit to man assessable in terms of this world. Yet worship is only possible because man is not a creature of this world and because he is a child of God and destined to be an inheritor of the kingdom of Heaven. Worship is the characteristic activity of Heaven and of all those whom God has called to their places there. A justification of worship on the grounds that it makes man more at home in this world, even if on the highest plane, is bound not only to fail, but to deceive. This is not to deny that the practice of worship enables a man the better to realize his role in this world as a stranger and a pilgrim who in a place of change and decay seeks a 'city which hath foundations'. But it only has these results when the eyes of the worshipper are fixed in faith upon that city and its Maker and not upon himself as existing independently of his eternal destiny.

It has been said above that the champions of the need for public worship have been thrown upon the defensive owing to the widespread attack upon its necessity. This is especially true of us clergy to whom falls the ordering of public worship. We are conscious of presiding over an activity whose usefulness is called in question, even among the most faithful of the habitual worshippers in our parishes. We have allowed ourselves to become nervous, and unconsciously we have become ready to make concessions even to views which we know in our hearts to be shallow and unsound. We do not wish to 'drive people away' by an unsympathetic handling of the matter, and sometimes we adopt practices which look very like 'appeasement'. As the size of a congregation is too often regarded as a thermometer registering the spiritual efficacy of the parson's work, he may get alarmed if it is not large. And this alarm may lead him to order his church services primarily with a view to increasing the congregation. Without knowing it he ceases to try to make worship acceptable to God or to order it in accordance with the mind of the Church. He is more concerned with filling the pews. He takes upon himself all the anxious concern of the theatre manager whose box-office receipts are dwindling and, though it may be of a high order, it is nevertheless entertainment and not public worship that he finds himself planning.

Another priest, confronted with much ignorance of the nature of worship and still more perhaps of the nature of the Christian faith will be tempted to regard the whole period of Divine service as an opportunity for instruction. The materials of public worship, hymns, psalms, Bible readings, prayers and sermon will all be chosen and manipulated in the effort to drive home one point of Christian teaching. Though the prayers are technically still addressed to God, it is their probable effect on the congregation which influences their selection, and the same will apply to other parts of the service. This kind of effort may first be made on some special occasion such as 'Industrial' Sunday, 'Farm' Sunday, Remembrance Day and so on. It is hoped to have a large attendance including many who are normally strangers to the pew. And therefore every effort will be made to hold the attention of this gathering and even to convince it that Christianity is relevant to human needs and everyday concerns. Without doubt evidence justifying this hope will be forthcoming after the service. Someone who has not been to church for years will say that if only church services were always like that he would be a regular churchgoer. Such testimony is stimulating and the clergyman responsible, actuated by genuine missionary zeal, will seek for ways in which his ordinary Sunday services may take on the character of the special service which has made so strong an impression. In view of what he feels to be a great opportunity he will consider himself free within fairly wide limits to adapt and modify the authorized rite so as to make each service sound some special note, plain and intelligible, to his congregation. These special 'notes' may be announced beforehand in the parish magazine or in the local press, and for a time at least, if he does it well, there will be a quickening of local interest in the new venture at St. X's. But it is not easy to go on doing this kind of thing well. The fact is that the traditional materials of public worship, psalm, collect and Bible lesson, do not lend themselves very easily to this mode of treatment. Anyone who has tried to arrange special services designed to give the Christian message for all sorts of human concerns will have met a certain stubborn resistance in Holy Scripture to this kind of manipulation. The Bible is either silent on many questions which occupy our minds or else speaks very ambiguously about them, mingling its halting references to the subject in hand with other material not at all to our purpose. As time goes on it becomes harder and harder to ring the changes and to compose a really relevant sequence of psalms, lessons and prayers suitable for the ends desired. After a while the clergyman begins to lose heart and to fall back more and more upon the sermon and perhaps some of the hymns. The service itself becomes regarded as a sort of 'softening' process preparing the mind to receive the teaching of the sermon. In the end he is back where he started.

And yet not quite where he started. In fact he has made it harder for his people to realize what worship really is. He has taught them to regard it as instruction, a means for infusing ideas. He has taught them that liturgy ought to come down to our level and meet us where we are. And yet he now finds himself unable to continue presenting it in that aspect. All he can do now is to prune the ordinary Prayer Book service of those elements which he supposes the people won't understand and possibly also to shorten it. Yet though he shortens the actual Prayer Book service, the total time spent in church may not be appreciably less. For every psalm he omits there will be a hymn inserted. Exhortations may be banished, but their place is taken by a number of prayers dealing with homely concerns and questions of the day. But even now perhaps he has not begun to teach his people really to worship. He has failed to justify public worship: he has merely succeeded in employing the time formerly occupied by public worship in doing something else.

Much of what has here been written is caricature. Probably no one person ever does exactly what the clergyman has above been described as doing. And yet in varying degrees the modern criticism of public worship is apt to be met in those ways. There is a strong and wide tendency to try to justify public worship in ways which in the end do not justify it. This will always be the case when public worship is regarded as a means to some immediate end and not as an end in itself. This in fact is the first assertion that must be made in the justification of public worship. It is an activity which is its own justification. Its principal value is in the actual doing of it, and not in such results as may be from time to time apparent. To worship is to be true to oneself as one made in the image of God. Worship is the inevitable response to an objective situation. Just as a man thinks because he is a rational being, so a man worships because he is a child of God, called to an eternal destiny in God's Kingdom. A man may stifle or even atrophy his power of reason, but in doing so he becomes not more, but less, true to his nature. So a man may stifle or even atrophy his power of worship, but in doing so he becomes false to his nature. Because God made him and because God calls him to eternal fellowship with Himself, therefore man must worship.

The activity of worship may however be diverted from its

lawful end. It is possible to worship false gods, and what is less than God. We, who are given the power to love, in order that we may love God, and both ourselves and other people *in* God, may nevertheless set our love upon ourselves and others as existing apart from God. In the same way a man may divert his powers of worship away from God and set it upon himself or even upon the State.[1] For people who know nothing about the true God, or who, though knowing God, are not interested in Him, may still worship. For the fact that such worship is not directed to its true end does not prevent its being real worship. But worship of what is less than God, or opposed to God, though real, is harmful. Therefore it is essential that man shall learn to worship the true God and to give his homage where it rightly belongs. For to worship is to acknowledge with every part of one's being the worth-ship of what is worshipped, to acknowledge with the mind, the affections and the will, its utter perfection. To commit oneself *thus* towards what is imperfect or perishable is to engender the lie in the soul: while *thus* to render homage to what objectively claims it, namely Almighty God, is to take one's appointed place in the Universe and to do what each one of us was born to do.

Such worship must be public as well as private, in consort with others as well as in solitude. For man is not acting true to the real situation of his humanity if he insists upon restricting his worship to occasions of isolation from his neighbour. His acknowledgement of God's sovereignty and holiness will be perilously defective if it is normally offered only in an artificial separation from his brother man. Though each of us is conceivable as a distinct individual, none of us is self-sufficient: the individual needs fellowship with others in the process of becoming his own self and achieving true humanity. Deliberately to assert one's isolation and lack of

[1] 'The seemingly endless line of poor young Germans containing a generation within its ranks, plodded steadily forward to kiss the hand of the Destroyer and to pay homage to the enemy of their country, their civilization, and their immortal souls.' *From a newspaper account of a Communist Youth Rally in East Berlin.*

## THE JUSTIFICATION OF PUBLIC WORSHIP 15

need for human fellowship at the supreme moment of worship is to give rein to that fatal arrogance which is the root of all human sin. True worship cannot co-exist with that failure in humility which shrinks from being one of a crowd. This is especially true of Christian worship, which is based upon the new covenant in Christ's blood, by which a new race of men is born, in which each member is related, not only to the Redeemer Himself, but to every other member of that race. A Christian congregation is not a fortuitous collection of individuals, moved to worship, but a living cell within that organism called by St. Paul the Body of Christ and likened by our Lord Himself to a Vine. Membership of that Body, or being a part of that Vine, is an indispensable condition of man's destiny in Christ. To worship God only in solitude is to reject that condition and deliberately to cling to a condition from which Christ came to save us.

When asked by the first disciples to teach them to pray, the Lord replied by giving them a prayer which begins *Our* Father. To use this prayer, and yet rigidly to insist upon never saying it with others is an odd way of honouring the authority of its Author. A proper and effective acknowledgement of God in worship cannot proceed from a man who believes that in things spiritual he has a duty to keep himself to himself. He must come down from his high horse and take his place with the multitude. True Christian worship should certainly be offered by every man in private, but it must also be offered in public, in association with the other members of the Body if it is to be true to its Christian character.

Further, Christian worship must also be consciously offered not only in union with other churchmen but in union with Christ. Where two or three are gathered together, there is He. It is only because of His presence in our midst that we are able really to worship the Father. And His presence in our midst is the result of what He has accomplished for us in His death and resurrection. Only in virtue of that, and of our consequent union with Him in Baptism, can our worship be availing. Christ alone from the human side has offered (and still offers) worship acceptable to the Father, and our worship can only be acceptable in and with His. The constantly recurring formula 'through Jesus Christ our Lord' is not a mere liturgical convention but the expression of the fundamental nature of what we are doing, without which our worship would be valueless. In a Christian assembly Christ holds the initiative in worship and it is our task to join in His prayer, for there is no other acceptable or efficacious prayer to join with.

That is why the Holy Communion is the centre and climax of Christian worship and why all other forms and methods of worship derive their adequacy from it. In that rite there is a proclamation before the Father and before men of that death through which alone sinful man can approach Holy God. In that rite there is a true and objective participation in, or communion with, the Body and Blood of Christ by which we are enabled to worship adequately, with a true self-oblation, the Father who seeks man's worship.

Christian worship then is far more than the bare acknowledgement by the individual of the worth-ship of God with which this brief analysis began. It is above all things a communal action, involving not merely a visible gathering of men, but the real and objective presence of the Son of God Himself, with whom also are joined the unseen members of the One Body whether in this world or in the world to come.

Because then public worship is a shared activity, its outward form is for the most part a form of words and actions consented to by the Church, as adequately expressing the mind of the Church in obedience to the guidance of the Holy Spirit. An individual Christian coming to church comes not so much to offer worship as to join in an offering continually going on. He comes not to initiate worship but to contribute to, and be carried up by, a worship which never ceases, the source and fountain of which lies in the eternal activity of Christ. He will not therefore expect to dominate the proceedings himself, nor hope that his own private needs and

## THE JUSTIFICATION OF PUBLIC WORSHIP

aspirations will receive priority of attention. He knows that the experience and understanding of the whole Church is far wider and deeper than his own and he will expect to profit by it and be led by it into paths and regions of adoration and praise which by himself he would never have found. Such advantages are secured for him by the liturgy of the Church in which materials for his worship, both old and new, are brought out of the Church's treasure house.

One reason why people find church services unhelpful may be that they have never been told that worship is active and not passive. People have got it into their heads that the business of church-going is largely confined to the receiving of impressions, to being edified, touched, moved, stimulated. They have not been told that they have come to work, and to contribute their understanding and their devotion in a positive, active way. Not having been told this they 'get it all wrong' and criticize the liturgy for not doing what it never set out to do.

Finally, public worship is to be justified on the grounds that it is a preparation for eternity. Christianity is not merely a religion to live by in this world, but a religion to die by. We are put into this world in order to learn what to set our hearts upon. In the world to come God has prepared good things for us, but they will only be considered good by those who have trained themselves here to want them. The conditions of life below are such as to give man all the knowledge he needs to distinguish between what is to be desired and what is to be shunned. Heaven could only be heaven to those who begin here to hunger for heavenly things. Public worship is a deliberate corporate act of desire for God and for what God offers. It is a formal exercise in delighting in the Lord. Because heaven may best be understood by us as a City, we can best prepare for it by learning *as a community* to delight in the Lord. Outside the hours of worship it is all too possible to forget God and to slip imperceptibly into a complacence with things as they seem to our senses to be, a condition which the Scriptures liken to 'darkness'. If we are to be ready for that other world, in which the presence of God will be inescapable, we must continually exercise ourselves in the art of realizing that presence now. We need frequent effort to get used to that almost unimaginable moment when, that God knows us, will be more vivid to our consciousness than our knowledge of Him. The occasion for that effort is public worship.

## 11

# THE BACKGROUND OF PUBLIC WORSHIP

WORSHIP is man's acknowledgement of the worth-ship of God with every part of his being. But this acknowledgement is insincere and meaningless unless he honours it in action. 'Truth,' wrote Father R. M. Benson, 'always requires subsequent action. It can never be known as a mere contemplation. It must be known interiorly so that a man may do it, act true to it.'

What is it then that man contemplates and acknowledges in God? First that He is Lord, that He is all-sovereign. This means that man's acknowledgement in worship must pass into a readiness to offer the homage of obedience. To acknowledge sincerely the worth-ship of God's sovereignty must imply an inner compulsion to correspond with the will of God, a movement towards compliance. If not, God's sovereignty has no real meaning and cannot be worth anything. To acknowledge that it has supreme value must be followed by obedience in action. This obedience is part of the worship.

But God who is sovereign is also Love. It is in the very nature of love that it requires a loving response. Love demands love in return. To acknowledge the worth-ship of perfect love is to acknowledge the rightness of its claim to be loved. A man who worships Him whom he believes to be Love cannot avoid the knowledge that if he too is to be worth anything he must love God in return. Love here is used in the New Testament sense of *agapē* or *caritas* (charity) and not in the most usual modern sense which implies primarily emotion or feeling. Charity fundamentally concerns not the feelings but the will: it is not at any rate at first a question of heightened affection, but rather of that activity known as 'self-giving'. Affection cannot be called into being by desire or effort, but love in the Christian sense can. 'Thou shalt love the Lord thy God' is a command which it is possible to begin to obey. Because God is Love and goes out in love to his children, the worshipper knows that love expressed in self-giving must be his own lawful and inevitable response to God. Again to acknowledge the worth-ship of divine love and yet to withhold the offering of self is to make worship unreal. Because God is worshipped, man must honour his worship by the obedience of self-giving love.

But this is just what man, unaided, cannot do, for he is sinful. His sinfulness inhibits his powers of obedience, pollutes his love, and makes his worship unacceptable. It is not possible in the space here allowed to dwell on this at length and I will content myself with quoting a classical definition.[1]

> 'Sin is an easy thing to us; we think little of it; we do not understand how the Creator can think much of it.... But consider what it is in itself; it is rebellion against God; it is a traitor's act who aims at the overthrow and death of his sovereign; it is that, if I may use a strong expression, which, could the Divine Governor of the world cease to be, would be sufficient to bring it about. It is the mortal enemy of the All-holy, so that He and it cannot be together; and as the All-holy drives it from His presence into the outer darkness, so, if God could be less than God, it would have power to make Him so.'

For this reason man, alone, cannot offer God a worship which he can accept. The worship of perfect love must imply a self-giving; self-giving implies a drawing near of him who is a sinner to the holiness of God. But this cannot be as long as man is in his sin. God cannot 'let a man off' from

[1] J. H. Newman, 'The Mental Sufferings of our Lord in His Passion'—the sixteenth sermon in *Discourses to Mixed Congregations*.

his sin, for sin is not an outward condition, but an inner personal disorder. In everyday relationships we have experience of this. If you do something evil to a friend, something antagonistic to that mutual relation of trust and respect, you thereafter instinctively avoid his presence. Your sin has erected a moral barrier between you. This is by no means removed if your friend happens to say: 'there's nothing to forgive'; the personal relationship between you is impaired in an inward spiritual way and may be ruined beyond hope of repair.

In some such way human sin cuts a man off from God and prevents his offering any worship which means anything. And because man is in the grip of sin, because he is afflicted with an inner condition of sinfulness of which by his own efforts he cannot get rid, he loses his appointed place in God's universe and gravitates towards that outer darkness of isolation to which sin logically leads him.

The Gospel, the good news, is that a way of salvation from this dilemma has been achieved by Christ. The Son of God has taken human nature upon Himself, and in it, within history and human life, has offered the Father perfect worship. Christ's work on earth was to do Himself what man so far had failed to do, to accomplish in human nature what the Father demanded, but what He had thus far failed to receive: to offer in fact acceptable worship. 'I have glorified thee on the earth,' said our Lord to His Father on the eve of His crucifixion, 'having accomplished the work which thou hast given me to do.'[2] The content and nature of this glorifying were revealed in his unbroken loyalty to the Father's sovereignty ('My meat is to do the will of him that sent me'[3]) offered in loving self-giving. His life was lived in a genuine human nature 'towards' the Father: every thought, word and deed was an honouring of this inner acknowledgement of the Father's sovereignty and love. In short His life was perfect worship.

Because, though Son of God, He yet allowed His divinity

[2] John 17.4.     [3] John 4.34.

to be limited by His real humanity, He (voluntarily) needed special times and places for intensive or ritual prayer and worship; we read of Him both attending the public worship of the Synagogue and the Temple, and retiring into quiet places for solitary prayer. The evidence of His meditation upon the Scriptures (the Old Testament) appears on almost every page of the Gospels. All this was an essential part of that one perfect act of worship of which His life consists.

Such a life drew upon Him the antagonism of the evil in man. Sin has been described above as 'that which, could the Divine Governor of the world cease to be, would be sufficient to bring it about'. The truth of these words is terribly illustrated in the Passion of Christ. Finding in their midst the holy and sinless Son of God, the hearts of average men, possessed by sin, converge upon Him in an unison of malicious antagonism. 'This is the heir; come, let us kill him, and take his inheritance.'[4] Never were all degrees of men of so many varying interests more compactly united than those who directly or indirectly brought about Christ's death. They were united by one common factor, sin, of which the very nature is that it strikes at God as at an enemy. And the Son of God receives their violence as materials for His worship. Ever since His presence at the Passover as a boy He has known with increasing clearness that His Father's business for Him is bound up with the shedding of His blood. He went to Jerusalem to meet it. Because He is in the midst of sinful men, 'it is written' that He must suffer. The suffering on the Cross is the climax of His self-offering in worship of the Father. 'Princes have persecuted me without a cause: but my heart standeth in awe of thy word.'[5] Whatever is done, He accepts it and offers up His faithful endurance thereof as His worship, never deviating from His love for the Father and for the very men who aim at His destruction. He is the faithful witness, and His self-giving is the pure-offering spoken of by Malachi.[6] Just before He breathed His last, He uttered the words (possibly in the 'loud cry' recorded by Luke),

[4] Matt. 21.38.  [5] Ps. 119.161.  [6] Mal. 1.11.

'It is finished' or, as it might be translated, 'It is accomplished'. The perfect worship of God has been offered in human nature.

But this perfect worship, though offered *to* the Father, is offered *for* man. 'For man' not in the sense of making it unnecessary for man any longer to try to worship, but in the sense of initiating a process in which even sinful man could now play his part. Christ's perfect worship is not accepted in default of our worship, but His worship can become the vehicle of our worship, the means by which our worship can reach acceptably the Throne of grace, and be progressively purified and perfected.

It appears to have been our Lord's sustained desire to associate men with what He was doing for them. This is seen clearly in at least two outstanding stages in His work of redemption, the Transfiguration and the agony in Gethsemane. Both these occasions were closely associated with His approaching death and on both our Lord was engaged in that formal and intensive worship which we call prayer. Yet although our Lord was doing what no sinful man could do, and doing it 'towards' the Father, on both occasions He is careful to take with Him three of His apostles. Though at the Transfiguration no words of Jesus are recorded in explanation to His apostles why He has brought them, in Gethsemane He urgently calls upon them to watch and pray with Him. He desired that His followers should, as far as they might, participate in what He was doing and be drawn into His own self-offering. In the Last Supper is shown more strikingly still the Lord's desire to gather men into His action. His ritual use of the bread and the cup during this supper has been described[7] as 'the giving of a triple pledge; to Himself, that what He had to do to-morrow He would accomplish ... to His Father, that the cup for all its bitterness should be drunk to the dregs' but, notice also, 'to His apostles, that "I appoint unto you a kingdom, as my Father hath appointed unto me; that ye may eat and drink at my table in my

[7] Gregory Dix, *The Shape of the Liturgy*, p. 76.

Kingdom ".' Thus our Lord makes clear, that, though He does for man what he could never do for Himself, man must nevertheless not be content to sit back as a mere passive recipient of benefits but, so far as is lawful for him, become identified with Christ's action and offer himself in and with his Lord. It is in this sense that our Lord says to men 'Come unto me' and 'Abide in me'. They are to come into a more intimate relation with Him than merely being within earshot: they are to be drawn into a unity as close as branches are with the vine, so that all that Christ is, becomes theirs, and in all that Christ does, they share. But what Christ does is to offer perfect worship: this offering is for man because man is at last able *in Christ* to fulfil his own destiny by joining in that worship.

The Resurrection and Ascension of our Lord are the Father's signs that the worship of Christ is accepted by Him, and that the new way to God is now open to man. When Christ entered the heavenly places at His Ascension He enters it still clothed in our humanity: human nature was brought by the Son of God into that Holy of Holies from which sin had hitherto excluded it: man is at last brought face to face with God. All this is strikingly related in the symbolic imagery of the Revelation of S. John the Divine. When the first vision of God is there described, the Almighty is shown surrounded by the heavenly court, but in front is 'the sea of glass like unto crystal'.[8] No human being is seen in heaven, for the sea represents that barrier which man's sin has erected, and the consequent wrath of God upon man. In a later vision 'there was no more sea'[9] for the Lion of the tribe of Judah had prevailed, the barrier between God and man had been broken down, and the way to God is open through Jesus Christ our Lord. 'The tabernacle of God is with men and he will dwell with them and they shall be his people.'[10]

To sum up then: we cannot have access to our Father in heaven, in prayer or worship, in our own right as human beings. We have lost that right. Only in virtue of what

[8] Rev. 4.6.     [9] Rev. 21.1.     [10] Rev. 21.3.

Christ has done are we able to come into the presence of God. Only so far as we are allowed to share Christ's sonship of the Father can we approach Him as sons should do. This is the great evangelical teaching which we perhaps do not hear as often as we used, but which is enshrined in hymns which are popular still, though too often sung parrot-fashion.

> Jesu, lover of my soul,
> Let me to thy bosom fly,
>
> . . . . .
> Hide me, O my Saviour, hide,
>
> . . . . .
> Other refuge have I none.
>
> \*
>
> Just as I am, without one plea
> But that thy Blood was shed for me
>
> . . . . .
> O Lamb of God, I come.
>
> \*
>
> Look Father, look on his anointed face,
> And only look on us as found in him.

We have to realize, when we have the urge to pray, that there is only *one* prayer in heaven or earth which prevails with God, the prayer of Him 'who in the days of his flesh . . . offered up prayers and supplications with strong crying and tears unto him that was able to save him from death, and was heard in that he feared.'[11] Unless we join in *that* prayer we cannot be heard—the prayer of our High Priest who prays on our behalf. That is why the prayers in all the classic liturgies of Christendom are explicitly offered only 'through Jesus Christ our Lord'.

Human language, admirably adapted to meet the needs of so many human concerns, ceases to be precise when the attempt is made to describe what is transcendental. It may well be that much of what has been written here has given the impres-

[11] Heb. 5.7.

sion that the work of Christ is something wholly outside, and even over against, the Godhead. It is only too easy when endeavouring to expound the mystery of salvation to speak of our Lord as though He were some pagan demi-god who stormed heaven, independently of the will of the Father, confronting Him with a *coup d'état*. But the Son of God is not a being in any way *separable* from the eternal Father though He is *distinct* from Him. When we pray and worship *in* Christ we must not think of our Lord as the Good Shepherd bringing His sheep to their true home to the great embarrassment of our Father in heaven. For as S. Paul says: 'God was in Christ reconciling the world unto himself.' To put it crudely the Father is 'a party' to all the work of Christ who, as the writer of the Fourth Gospel attests, said, 'The Son can do nothing of himself, but what he seeth the Father do: for what things soever he doeth, these also doeth the Son likewise.'[12]

All this presents great difficulties to our imagination. It is not, however, the purpose of this book to expound the doctrine of the Blessed Trinity, but only to indicate how in fact this doctrine is deeply implied in any possible analysis of the nature of worship. Because it is only through the Holy Spirit that we can have faith in Christ and because only in Christ can we approach the Father, all prayer and worship is a sharing in the life of God. Within the Being of God there is love given and love received, adoration offered and adoration accepted. When Christians worship, they are drawn into this timeless and eternal activity, which goes on whether they join in or not. In worship we are taken up into God and allowed to live His life. An attempt has been made here to speak of this venture in stages of temporal succession: yet from first to last we are in God when we pray, and our activity is supernatural and ineffable. This is what we were made for: in worship we have a foretaste of our destiny. That is why we worship.

We need to get a conscious grip of these truths which

[12] John 5.19.

underlie the practice of prayer and worship. Too often we permit ourselves to think of worship with quite a different background: we think of it as an activity of our own human initiative. We think of ourselves perhaps, in a Christian congregation, as a forlorn group of men, stranded upon a desert island, endeavouring to attract the attention of a passing ship. It is our need which is the cause of what we do, and which may prevail upon the captain of the passing ship to turn aside from his pre-arranged course and to pay attention to us. Yet fundamentally the ground of worship is not human initiative: it is a response to a divine movement or call. The Father *seeks* men to worship Him in spirit and in truth. It is the essence of God's creative act that His creation shall worship Him, because in that worship the nature of both God and man is true to itself. So God draws men to worship Him. We may think that we have gone to church in order to dwell upon higher things, and to cultivate our soul, or to improve our moral ideal. But long before we ever conceived the notion of so doing 'the eyes of the Lord which run to and fro throughout the whole earth '[13] have seen us and He has begun to draw us to Himself in Christ by the Holy Spirit.

So worship is more than a mechanism for feeling good, more than an occasion for 'giving our vote for God' or setting a good example, more than a serious attention given to 'one above', more even than witness to truth or reception of grace: it is to be led into the Father's presence and to live the life of God.

Some notion of all this we must have if we are to worship with mind, heart, and will. We are not saved by knowledge, or by holding correct views. But the more we use the minds we have been given faithfully, and perseveringly, and humbly, the better we shall worship. We must worship in spirit, but we must also worship, as far as we can, in truth. We must at least be firmly aware of two things: that we could not worship at all, were it not for what Christ has done, and still does, in us; that because we may enter the Father's presence

[13] II Chron. 16.9.

in Christ, therefore to worship is to be encompassed by God and to share His life. The Church may indeed be unable to expound to our reason's complete satisfaction the mystery of the Godhead, and the mystery of how sinful man can have fellowship with Him who is of purer eyes than to behold iniquity. But in her worship she brings us into living contact with these mysteries, so that they become effective in us.

# III

# THE MATERIALS OF WORSHIP (1)

## Words

'The worshipper in public worship touches what is beyond himself in three respects. The first objective aspect is the sense of God's presence, the Being to whom devotion is given. . . . The second objective aspect is the presence of other lives, for worship in its origin and nature is a social act. . . . The third objective aspect is the means through which the worship is offered. . . . It is in every case something visible or audible that is not himself.'[1]

This third objective aspect is the subject of this and the following two chapters.

Even in these days of a very widespread ignorance of the Bible, a few texts are comparatively well known, among them being: 'God is a Spirit: and they that worship him must worship in spirit and truth.'[2] It is however doubtful if the words are as widely understood as they are remembered. It is commonly believed that these words enjoin a worship wholly independent of things that can be touched, seen or heard,

'that genuine worshippers of God are thereby "freed from every chain that binds men to the realm of the flesh, to sacred times and places and ceremonies"; that the truly religious man "obeys a purely inward spiritual worship of God".'[3]

---

[1] *Our Heritage in Public Worship*, D. H. Hislop (T. & T. Clark), p. 5.
[2] John 4.24.
[3] *The Fourth Gospel*, Sir Edwyn Hoskyns (Faber), Vol. I, p. 267.

It is further thought that worship 'in truth' means worship in accordance with the sincerely held convictions of the worshipper, whatever they may happen to be. Consequently it is very common to hear Quaker worship described as, of all known types of worship, that which most faithfully corresponds with our Lord's definition. It is held to be so, both because Quakers seek to be wholly independent of material *media* in their worship and because such words as are uttered are at any rate intended to be wholly unpremeditated. This view is held by many people, most of whom perhaps have no certain intention of ever associating themselves with Quaker worship.

Further, the word 'spiritual' is often thought, not only to imply as great a separation as may be from everything material, but also to imply a necessary goodness. There cannot exist, so it is thought, any thing or process in the spiritual realm which is not therefore completely good and trustworthy. As soon as a man, in so far as he can, escapes from the domination or the use of what is visible, audible or tangible, he must of necessity be on the right path which will sooner or later bring him into the presence of God. To those who hold such notions any discussion of 'the material' of worship is irrelevant. The very introduction of such a question is to abandon the possibility of worship in spirit and truth. Though its promoters might not describe it in such words, it is nevertheless true that such worship is all but the equivalent of escape.

To S. John, who gives us these words of our Lord about worship, such an interpretation would have been surprising. To him our Lord had taught something quite different in the words Spirit and spiritual.

> 'He who had spoken to Nicodemus of the Spiritual birth from above which is God's answer to baptism by water (John 3.5-6) now speaks to the woman of Samaria of the true worship of the Father, which is spiritual because it makes room for the reverse and corresponding action of God from above. This reverse operation and power of God is defined as Spirit. . . .

Without faith in the power of the Holy Spirit of God, all human worship is meaningless.'[4]

Spiritual worship is therefore not, in these words of our Lord, contrasted with worship which makes use of specified words, actions, or places, but with a worship which does not reach the true God.

> 'By the Incarnation men are enabled to have immediate communion with God, and thus a worship in spirit has become possible: at the same time the Son is a complete manifestation of God for men, and thus a worship in truth has been placed within their reach.'[5]

The use, then, of words, actions or special places in public worship is not condemned either in these or in any other words of our Lord. Spiritual worship is not confined to unexpressed aspiration or wordless contemplation, and has nothing at all to do with that vague and consoling religiosity with which it is so often confused.

Words are the most obvious use of material in public worship. Indeed where, as with Christians, worship is a social act, they are indispensable. If a number of human souls are to embark upon a common act there must be communication between them to ensure that the act is really shared. Public worship does not mean the simultaneous prayer of a number of people who are united only in the sense that they are spatially near one another. Public worship is a common offering involving heart, mind and will, so that words are necessary to ensure this.

But what sort of words? There are some who say that as we must worship 'in spirit', the actual words must be entirely and directly prompted by the Holy Spirit; that we must place ourselves in His hands and utter only such words as there and then He puts into our hearts. This means that the words used in public worship must be un-premeditated and that only so will worship be spiritual. To use pre-arranged formulæ

[4] Hoskyns, *op. cit.*, p. 259.
[5] *The Gospel According to S. John*, B. F. Westcott (John Murray), p. 73.

is to forsake that reliance upon the Holy Spirit which must be the guiding principle. To 'pray with the Spirit' is to eliminate the human factors of thought and aspiration, and to let the Holy Spirit utter what He will through us.

But the Holy Spirit does not work in man by suppressing or by-passing all that is human, and replacing it by what is purely divine. The guidance of the Holy Spirit is not a process by which God saves us from thinking and supplies right thoughts ready-made. The mode of His operation is rather to quicken and stimulate our thoughts, intentions, and desires at their best, and to lead them on from these further than we, unaided, could go; to make the best of such material as we can offer, and to transform it. As has been well said, 'God hath sent forth the Spirit of the Son into our hearts (not into our tongues) whereby we cry Abba, Father.' To worship God in words which are the fruit of thought and deliberation cannot be less spiritual than to address Him without reflection. Unless all human processes of thought, consideration, and imagination are totally corrupt and unredeemable we are bound to put ourselves into the Divine hands only after we have done our best with human art and ingenuity. Can we do our best if we always leave it to the last moment?

S. Paul was much concerned with a mysterious faculty called 'speaking in a tongue' which seems to have been common,[6] at any rate in the Corinthian Church. This faculty, which S. Paul recognized as God-given, found its outlet at times of public worship when men felt called, not only to speak 'in a tongue', but to pray 'in a tongue'. Such prayer was undoubtedly 'with the spirit', but S. Paul deprecated its use in public worship because, being divorced from the understanding, it did not serve the common purpose at such a time. Though S. Paul himself possessed this faculty he could yet say 'Howbeit in the church I had rather speak five words with my understanding, that I might instruct others also, than ten thousand words "in a tongue"' (I Cor. 14.19). For

[6] This would be now called a sort of gibberish.

him, praying with the understanding was not inconsistent with reliance upon the Holy Spirit.

But it is not given to everyone to pray with the understanding *extempore*, indeed the gift is rare and probably always has been. George Eliot, no friend to the Anglican Church, records:

> 'I enjoyed the fine selection of Collects he (the Unitarian minister) read from the Liturgy. What an age of earnest faith, grasping a noble conception of life, and determined to bring all things into harmony with it, has recorded itself in the simple, pregnant, rhythmical English of these Collects and of the Bible. The contrast when the good man got into the pulpit and began to pray in a borrowed, washy lingo—*extempore* in more senses than one.'[7]

Many years previously Jeremy Taylor had critically referred to 'those unhandsome issues of a sudden tongue', and we have all had experiences of a similar distaste. That it is impossible to utter prayer which is both 'with understanding' and yet un-premeditated, is not asserted, but its occurrence is infrequent enough to forbid reliance upon it as a necessity of public worship.

And however excellent such *extempore* prayer can be, there is a further reason why it cannot provide the staple diet for the 'reasonable service' of public worship. Common prayer includes a collective effort of each to make the words of the minister his own. It needs attentiveness: the words of the service must be appropriated by each worshipper so that he can contribute through them his own quota of devotion to the common act. When the officiant prays *extempore* nobody knows what is coming next. Each must carefully listen, but before he is able to digest and make an adequate offering of what he hears, the minister has passed on to another phrase, thus throwing the thoughts of the attentive worshipper into confusion. It is often all but impossible to keep pace with the utterer of *extempore* prayer. The result frequently is that

[7] *Life of George Eliot*, Vol. II, p. 264.

the individual worshipper merely *listens* to the prayer of the minister without entering into more than the very general sense of it. Indeed worshippers have been seen on such occasions sitting back in their pews with folded arms, engaged apparently in merely appraising the efforts of the minister.

It is therefore claimed that pre-meditated prayer, set forth in forms accessible to the congregation—and therefore either printed or known by heart—is from a practical point of view the most suitable medium for public worship, if that worship is to be offered with the understanding. Such prayer would seem always from the first to have been at least an element in Christian public worship. The provision by our Lord of the form of words known as the Lord's Prayer set the Divine approval upon fixed forms. Both the Epistles and the Gospels contain embedded in their texts forms of words which scholars tell us represent primitive liturgical prayer: e.g. 'Awake thou that sleepest, and arise from the dead and Christ shall shine upon thee' (Eph. 5.14) and 'For if we died with him, we shall also live with him,' etc. (II Tim. 2.11). It is indeed hardly likely that the apostles brought up in the liturgical tradition of the Synagogue, would have abruptly abandoned a method of public worship to which they were accustomed, in default of express prohibition by our Lord. In that tradition extemporaneous prayer was also permissive and it is not therefore surprising that this method too should have persisted within the new Covenant, to which fact Justin Martyr, for instance, attests when he speaks of the President at the Eucharist as 'sending up prayer and thanksgiving likewise to the best of his ability'. Whether the eventual eclipse of *extempore* prayer reflects a decrease of spiritual vitality, or a belief that fixed forms were more practical and salutary, the reader must now decide for himself.

Quite apart from the difficulty of maintaining, year in and year out, a practice of prayer which is both un-premeditated and yet 'with the understanding', there are very important reasons for encouraging fixed forms. It is essential that every local congregation shall realize that it does not worship in isolation from the rest of the Church, whether on earth or in paradise, and also that it worships in and through a Being other than itself, Christ, the Head of the Church. Public worship must always be understood, not as the human initiation of a process in one corner of the earth, but rather as a joining in something always going on, both throughout the Church on earth and eternally in the heavenly places. A 'given' liturgy is a constant reminder of that fact. Those whose faith in the reality of the Church is weak are always demanding that a religious service shall express more or less exactly their own notions and aspirations, and must contain nothing that does not obviously and in detail meet their conscious demands. The liturgy, in other words, must come down to their level if it is to be of service to them. 'There was not a word about the atomic bomb,' said a man in dispraise of a service he had attended.

But a consciousness that the congregation of which I am a member is only one of tens of thousands on the earth's surface, and is as a drop in a bucket among the myriads in the world to come, makes me less clamorous that my momentary pre-occupations shall dominate the concern of all at public worship. I want rather, not a liturgy which comes down to my level, but one which will take me and my fellow worshippers out of ourselves and our little world into a vaster experience of God than ever I can imagine with my modest spiritual resources. A fixed liturgy, gloriously indifferent to my worries and notions, not hedged about with the limitations of life in my neighbourhood or the decade in which I live, is going to do for me just what needs doing. It will confront me with the eternal verities and place me upon the everlasting hills; I shall realize that my thoughts are not God's thoughts nor His ways mine; and then I may begin with angels and archangels to worship and adore. Having done this, I can view the atomic bomb and the election to the City Council in a more balanced perspective. In theory this could no doubt be achieved under the spiritual guidance of an offerer of *extempore* prayer, but he would have to be of the calibre of S. Paul or S. Augustine. A fixed liturgy with a long and steady growth behind it, slowly evolved through the centuries, with its roots in early antiquity, not too strongly betraying the special pre-occupations of any one epoch of history, is the ideal material for public worship.

A fixed liturgy has a further benefit. Worship is at least a two-fold activity. It is partly the *expression* of a conscious homage and loving devotion, a directing of existing energies of faith, hope and love towards their proper goal. But it is also an activity which, under God, helps to call such energies into being in the heart and mind of the worshipper. 'I kiss my child,' it has been said, 'not only because I love it, but in order that I may love it.' In the same way I may join with other worshippers in the psalm-verse 'Whom have I in heaven but thee: and there is none upon earth that I desire in comparison of thee' (Ps. 73.24, Prayer Book version). At the time of utterance these words may evoke only a faint response within, they perhaps represent an over-expression of the faith and love then actually present. But the recital of these words may actually deepen my devotion provided I truly desire them to be an expression of my inward aspiration. The words of the liturgy thus act as a vehicle both of expression and also of aspiration. We bite off, as it were, more than we can chew. To assist in the Church's liturgy is like learning to play the piano. In order to play a Beethoven sonata you begin just by playing it and playing it very badly. But playing it badly helps you to play it better next time. If you waited till you could play it perfectly before setting your fingers to the keys you would never play it at all. In other words, worship must be both expression and *exercise*. In order to worship adequately you must begin by worshipping inadequately: by persisting in the exercise of worship you will grow to a more perfect worship.

But this requires a form of worship which is largely fixed like the music of a sonata. You might learn to play the piano by practising a different sonata every time you sat down to the piano and by never playing the same one twice. But it would be a very lengthy process and you would never get far advanced in the art. So with worship. If you always used different words every time you worshipped progress would be slow. It is the perseverance with a given form which enables you to learn how to worship and which helps you to advance in the art. The words of a liturgy can be compared also to the tools which a craftsman uses. Every workman likes to have his own tools. He gets to know them and to be able to overcome by practice any special defect in them. If he found a new set of tools at his bench every morning, his progress in his craft would be very much slower. So in worship we need familiar words if they are to be a satisfactory medium for worship. If worship be partly exercise, then the forms of worship should be constant and fixed in the main, though with room for variable elements. As the author of *Eikon Basilike* has observed: 'God is not more a God of variety than of constancy.'

If people realized this element of exercise in worship more clearly you would not hear it said so often 'There is so much in the church service that I cannot say sincerely'. A man may complain that it is unreal for him to call himself a miserable sinner because he does not feel he is. But the words are put before him, not to express what he actually at the moment feels, but to state the truth to the realization of which he must progressively aspire. It is this process which a fixed liturgy greatly assists: the 'growing up into' a perfect worship.

There is another considerable advantage in a fixed liturgy, though this very asset is often regarded as a liability. Being fixed it cannot be often or lightly revised. The result of this is that the doctrine and ethos of this liturgy will in no generation precisely accord with the prevailing 'climate of opinion' at that time. Each generation has its favourite doctrines and the tendency is to concentrate upon these, to the exclusion of others, and to wish to make public worship reflect prevailingly the theological pre-occupations of the hour. This means in practice the retaining in divine service of those elements which emphasize what is fashionable, and the eclipse or omission of what is not at the moment in favour. A fixed liturgy hinders this movement and not at all to the disadvantage of true religion. *Lex orandi lex credendi* or in other words the Church's prayer reflects the Church's faith. But the Church's faith is always larger and more profound than a single congregation or even a single generation can assimilate at once in due proportion. There will always be elements in divine revelation which 'mean less' to one generation than to another, and there will always be the tendency to regard what is easy to believe as being 'more fundamental' than what seems out of tune with the pre-occupations of the moment. To limit public worship to those elements in the liturgy which confirm and emphasize what we find congenial at present, and to prune out what appears to be unsympathetic or unedifying, or even unintelligible, is very short-sighted. It is like removing the distant landscape from a picture on the grounds that it is too far away and distracts us from the appreciation of the foreground. The value of a liturgy lies especially in its contrasts, in its theological light and shade, in its vast horizons, in the presence within it of 'things new and old'. To take from it all that is not of immediate interest and delight is both to impoverish and distort it. A generation which is struck by the wonder of God's benevolence and thereupon omits, or tones down in its liturgy all that speaks of God's wrath,[8] not only does violence to truth but actually emasculates the doctrine it favours, making it a flimsy, two-dimensional shadow of a truth. As Mr. C. S. Lewis has said:

> 'If our religion is something objective, then we must never avert our eyes from those elements in it which seem puzzling or repellent; for it will be precisely the puzzling or the repellent which conceals what we do not yet know, and need to know.'

A fixed liturgy assists and promotes this.

Not infrequently this tendency towards theological exclu-

[8] 'Save us from being blinded to Thy whole meaning by the brightness of some single utterance.' *Mysteries of the Mass in Reasoned Prayers.* W. Roche.

THE MATERIALS OF WORSHIP 39

siveness leads to another, namely to make public worship reflect, not merely the theological, but the secular philosophical fashions of the day. The motive for this is at best pastoral, for it springs from a wish to make a casual, non-Christian church-attender at least less antagonistic to the Christian Church. It is hoped that by judiciously pruning the liturgy, the ethos of Christian worship may appear more welcoming to the secularist and lead him on to a reconsideration of his faith or non-faith. But a fixed liturgy makes this process difficult to achieve, at any rate on a local level. Nor is this a drawback. To try to entice a non-believer by obscuring the 'whole counsel of God' is as fruitless as it is unprincipled, nor, it must be repeated, should an act of worship be primarily regarded as an instrument of evangelism. And further the secular climate of opinion is a continually shifting thing. What is fashionable to-day will be unfashionable to-morrow; the bait attached to the liturgical hook in one decade will have lost its savour in the next, even if it ever had any! There is always a 'scandal' or stumbling-block in Christian faith, and the liturgy, no less than the creeds, cannot rid themselves of it if they are to be true to divine revelation.

Finally, the chief reason for a fixed liturgy is that it can be regulated by authority. The words of a liturgy must be such that through their use the Church may enter into the mind of Christ through whom our prayers are carried into the presence of God. Words are the bridge between His mind and ours. As such they must be suited to this high purpose. A matter of such crucial importance should not be left to the individual minister. Like Creeds, liturgies should be determined by the authority of the Church, and this implies fixed forms.

But a fixed liturgy will lose most of its advantages if worshippers do not habitually fix their attention upon it while it is being recited or sung. In days gone by people seemed to realize this more than they do to-day, for it used to be far more general in Anglican churches for worshippers to follow the service in their Prayer Books and Bibles. To-day people are more commonly content merely to use their books for those portions of the service which are congregationally sung, i.e. for the psalms and for the hymns. During the rest of morning or evening prayer and often during the whole of the Communion Service, they are content to rely upon their memory for the people's part and to rely upon their ears for the priest's part. This is, of course, possible, but it imposes a very heavy strain upon such powers of attention and concentration as most of us have. It is so fatally easy to be distracted from the business in hand when in church. To follow the service, both in Prayer Book and Bible, with the eye, as well as with the ear and the memory, is a powerful remedy against such distraction and ensures a far more hearty participation in what is going on. How many of us are so much trained in the art of concentration that we can afford to dispense with our books if we are to take an intelligent and sustained part in the service?

It must be confessed, however, that the abandonment of books has come about because people are uncertain what the officiating minister will do next. The practice of omitting much in the Prayer Book service, and of inserting material from other sources, has grown so fast that in perhaps most churches the worshippers cannot follow the service in their books without a good deal of effort and nimbleness of mind. This has greatly discouraged the practice and has resulted in a habit of listlessness in church which is not to the advantage of worship. Clergymen who omit and interpolate should seriously ponder whether the advantages of what they do outweigh the loss caused by the inattention of the people who cannot then follow the service in their books.

For worship is work, not the mere receiving of impressions, and no work can be of much avail unless the mind be wholly in it. Perhaps there is no system of public worship which makes such heavy demands upon the attention of the humblest worshipper as does the Book of Common Prayer, but none either which is so uniquely rewarding of the effort to be attentive.

# IV

# THE MATERIALS OF WORSHIP (2)

## Music

THERE is no real controversy nowadays about the suitability of music to worship though there have been times when it was hotly debated. To-day music is universally regarded as a fit and proper medium of worship. Even so there is not universal agreement as to the grounds upon which music is desired in church. An accredited spokesman of an organization for the improvement of church music recently stated that 'music is not necessary to worship'. In a sense this is true, in the same way that two hands are not necessary for the life of a human being. It would indeed be possible to keep alive, and even enjoy life, with only one hand, yet this would be a maimed life, imperfect and incomplete. Even so is worship, without music, a truncated worship, needlessly limited and handicapped.

This is said with some trepidation, for Richard Hooker appears to take a different view. He accepts, and even champions, the mating of worship and music but seems inclined to do this as a concession to human frailty, as an expedient for beguiling 'dry and tough hearts' into the paths of religious aspiration. He quotes a passage from S. Basil's Commentary on the Psalms which seems to support him, concluding with this memorable exordium: 'O the wise conceit of that heavenly Teacher which hath by his skill found out a way, that doing those things wherein we delight we may also learn that whereby we profit.' In other words, music is the sugar on the pill! Certainly an excellent reason for employing music, but it must still be asked, though with deference, whether there is not a more profound reason.

There is a very important practical reason. When people meet together for worship, to offer a form of common prayer and praise, it is desirable that such common praise shall be vocal as well as unanimous. The body as well as the mind and the spirit should be involved, and as much of the body as possible. Speaking, as well as hearing and seeing. But community speech, if it is not to be a mere babel of sound, is a most difficult accomplishment. Even Cathedral Chapters at their daily offices in choir rarely achieve this art, and they are small groups compared with an average congregation. The easiest way for an assembly of people to unite in common utterance with dignity and intelligibility is by singing. The laws of song are simpler than the laws of speech: song is therefore the more practical means of a communal utterance of praise. This must be one reason why religious worship and singing have always been so closely associated.

But there is a more fundamental reason for this association. All true worship approaches towards ecstasy. Ecstasy means literally a 'standing out of oneself'. Worship is the attempt to stand out of myself and identify myself with what I am not yet. It is a reaching out, a going out of myself, from myself, towards Him who dwells in light that no man can approach unto. All true worship moves in this direction: even in its early stages it partakes to some extent of the nature of ecstasy. And music is the very language of ecstasy, the true expression in sound of the man who is taken out of himself. This must be the fundamental reason why worship and music go together, and always have gone together unless forcibly put asunder by some passing fashion of thought.

Everyone feels this essential congruity between worship and music when hymns or psalms are in question, and, more recently, in the singing of 'prose' portions of the Holy Communion service such as Nicene Creed, *Sanctus* and *Gloria in excelsis*. But many are dubious concerning the chanting of prayers and collects by the priests, and still more of the recital on a monotone by the whole congregation of elements in the service such as the General Confession at Mattins and Evensong. Similarly of the chanting with inflexions of Epistle and Gospel at the Eucharist, or the Lord's Prayer after the Communion of the people. In these latter instances people are apt to assert that it would be more seemly to use the 'natural voice'. This nervousness of doing anything unnatural is never very far away when people get inside church. Insincerity in worship is something we justly dread. The abandonment of the 'natural voice' is suspected to be a move away from sincerity.

But the word 'natural' wants closer examination. It easily promotes confusion of thought. It is often used as a synonym for 'habitual'. To speak of a process coming natural to a man usually refers to something he does easily because he is used to it. Thus to many the 'natural voice' means using the voice as one commonly uses it in conversation; that is to say, vocal utterance in which the pitch is rapidly and irregularly varied. If this be exclusively the natural voice, then of course the chant of the priest or a recital in monotone by a choir and congregation is un-natural. But it is not true that 'natural' is the equivalent of 'habitual'. A man acts naturally, not necessarily when he acts as he usually does, but when he acts in a manner true to the laws of his being. In conversation it is natural to speak at a rapidly and irregularly varying pitch. But worship is different from conversation. It is on another level. Worship is the approach to ecstasy, and at this level it is natural to find a different type of vocal utterance from that employed in intimate or casual conversation. Even in conversation one can note differences. For instance, a man is explaining his conduct to another who has criticized it. Sooner or later he makes some statement as: 'My dear friend, I assure you on my word of honour that——' As he says this, his voice quite perceptibly abandons the rapid variation of pitch hitherto used and begins to partake in some degree of the character of a solemn chant—slow, measured, and with a more even pitch. He is approaching ecstasy, he comes out of himself and becomes the spokesman of truth or honour: he is less personal, more universal. Such a tone need not be forced or un-natural. It is, in fact, natural to him at the moral level the talk has reached.

The point here elaborated would not have seemed so strange to earlier generations as it does commonly to ours. Anciently poetry was intended to be sung or chanted and was in fact so rendered. True poetry is ecstasy clothed in words. It would have seemed un-natural to read poetry aloud in the same style as a detective story is read aloud. Even as late as our grandfathers' or our fathers' time poetry was commonly read aloud in a style which verged upon a chant. But in recent times this practice has come to be dubbed as 'stagey', probably because it became abused by extending this method of utterance to literature which was not really poetry, or ecstasy, at all.

But the Church's liturgy is indeed akin to poetry and one should not expect the human utterance of it to be of the same style as when conversing. In the adoration of Almighty God it is natural that a man's utterance will become distinct and different from that employed on trivial business. The liturgical chant, with or without inflexions, is the form which countless generations of worshipping Christians have found to be a suitable and natural means of utterance *in the performance of public worship*.

It also has its practical value. Churches, even village churches, are comparatively large buildings. The rapid and irregular variation of pitch which is possible in intimate conversation becomes unpractical in a large building. The larger the church the greater the difficulty of hearing a man talking in a conversational voice, and the more the need of an utterance of little-varying pitch. Newsboys discover this in the streets where they accordingly announce their wares in a sing-song voice, not unlike an ecclesiastical chant. In earlier days this chant of the street-vendor actually burgeoned into melody and the street-cries of itinerant merchants became songs.

The utterance, then, of true worship in a public assembly, both from practical reasons, and on grounds of an inner spiritual necessity, takes the form of music. Normally this music will be congregational. It is desirable that in most churches most of the music shall be such as all can join in. But it is also right and proper that, where available, trained singers in a choir should sing a short portion of the service by themselves. A community should offer all its best gifts to God in worship and it is most desirable that those who are skilled in choral singing should have a chance of making their contribution, at least from time to time. Such singing should not dominate the musical parts of a service in an ordinary parish church, as seemed to be the ideal of many exuberant parish choirmasters forty or more years ago; but neither should such singing be totally banished where it can be had. A short anthem or a four-part setting of the Canticles at Evensong, or an *Agnus Dei* or motet at the Eucharist, sung well by a choir, can be a most valuable contribution to the worship of a congregation. In a great parish church of a city or county-town a little more can well be attempted. To maintain a variety of type is most important, though the norm will be congregational singing almost entirely led, where possible, by a choir.

It may not be considered valueless if something is said here about the traditional type of Anglican cathedral worship and its musical ideals. A cathedral church is normally served by a body of men, both clerical and lay, who constitute the cathedral Foundation. This Foundation has the duty of maintaining, as continuously and as magnificently as possible, the daily worship of God. The Foundation is essentially a brotherhood of prayer and the brotherhood includes the lay members, the vergers, singing men, and chorister boys, as well as the dignitaries and canons. The Foundation is thus a 'congregation' of Christian men whose first duty is to maintain the worship of God in the cathedral church. On behalf of the whole diocese the cathedral Foundation maintains this round of worship, an activity not possible on the same scale in the parish churches. The work of the bishop in guiding and ministering to his flock is thus encompassed, at the heart of the diocese, with daily prayer and praise.

Cathedral churches are normally planned on the most sumptuous architectural scale attainable, and every effort is made to enrich them in the most splendid manner that the arts of the sculptor, the carpenter, the glass-painter, and the weaver can command. Small wonder then if the art of the musician, the singer and the organ builder is added in order that the external quality of the worship offered shall be commensurate in scale with the excellence of the building itself.

And so it has come about that a tradition of elaborate musical expression has established itself quite naturally in these elaborately constructed temples of worship. The music is indeed so elaborate that it can only be maintained if the greater part of the Foundation present at daily worship consists of highly trained singers.

It is this rich tradition of choral music which is from time to time adversely criticized by the visitor possessed by egalitarian views. He is used himself to worshipping in a church where nearly all the music, quite rightly, is within the compass of the normal, and even the casual, worshipper. When he takes his place in the stalls of a cathedral for Evensong he finds himself compelled to be all but dumb throughout the service. He protests at this limitation and is apt to clamour that the whole vocal expression of worship shall be brought down to his own musical level. To him the inspired versatility of William Byrd and the sublime maturity of Orlando Gibbons count for nothing. He cares little for the labours of Boyce or Croft, Battishill, Greene or Walmisley; Purcell and Vaughan Williams are an abomination to him. They have committed an unforgivable sin: they have written something which 'I can't sing' and should therefore have no place in the worship of the house of God. He does not reflect that the music he dubs 'uncongregational' is really congregational when the nature of a cathedral congregation is remembered.

For a cathedral congregation is normally the cathedral Foundation of which skilled singers form the greater part. He does not reflect that if he had come in at Mattins, he might have been the only person present not wearing a surplice. For elaborately choral services are still sung whether visitors attend or no: the object of the music is not primarily to edify visitors but part of an offering made to Almighty God of the best of which human nature in that place is capable.

This may sound as though cathedral authorities care nothing for the presence of visitors at their daily choral service. Such is very far from the case. There is nothing more encouraging to the members of a cathedral Foundation than when people assemble to worship with them. Would to God that at every service a multitude of people would attend. But people who attend cathedral services must remember that they are present at a type of worship different from that to which they are accustomed. Ordinarily their own voices are the vehicles of their own praise. But when assisting at a cathedral or collegiate service the vehicle of their worship must be the voices of others. Spiritually they must learn to use the choir as their representatives and to make the singing by picked voices the outward expression of their own aspirations. This means that worshipping in a cathedral is in some ways harder work than worshipping in an ordinary church. It requires greater attention on the part of the worshipper: there are more occasions of distraction: the outward harmonies of the choir must be supported by the lifting up of the heart of the non-singing worshipper: to do this in a sustained effort is not at first easy. But it is well worth trying, as every cathedral canon knows. Is there a greater privilege on this earth than to worship day by day through the trained and disciplined voices of the singing members of the Foundation whose repertory includes some of the finest pieces of music ever uttered by the mind of man? It is true that he would often like to have something he could sing himself, but he knows that, if he follows the singing with the worship of his heart, the total offering to God can be something incomparably more precious than would be the case if the musical standard were levelled down to the capacity of the least gifted singer.

This consideration at once raises the question of plain-song. The almost complete absence in the cathedral tradition of that venerable form of choral singing is a matter for regret. As things stand Anglican cathedral music begins only in the sixteenth century. Except in half-hidden ways, the staple ecclesiastical music of earlier generations is in many places almost unrepresented; the ancient melodies which ascended from the choir stalls when their wooden canopies were first carved and when the stone vault overhead was new, are for the most part no longer heard. Yet for at least three reasons the use of a considerable amount of plain-song would be a great gain in cathedral worship.

First of all plain-song conveys most strikingly a sense of the past; its regular day to day use builds up a sense of continuity with the past. Christian worship gains in depth wherever it is emphasized that the actual visible congregation is only a fragment of something far larger, that all congregations, though separated by space, are yet one worshipping body engaged in one eternal act. It gains still more when this sense of unity transcending space is realized also as a unity transcending time. In a completely real sense the worship in a particular place on a particular day is one with all other acts of worship in previous ages. Everything therefore in the outward forms of worship which can emphasize this fact of unity with the past can widen and deepen the quality of worship offered and is of immense value. In music, plain-song perhaps conveys this more eloquently than any other style of singing. After Evensong at a cathedral in which the canticles had been sung to a setting in which harmonic music alternated with plain-song verses, a man once said to me: 'Didn't you feel the saints beginning to stir when the plain-song began?'

Secondly, there is a quality in plain-song which makes even non-critical people realize that it is religious music. This is frequently apparent on the stage or film. When religious emotion is to be realized or a setting given to some ecclesiastical happening, music of a modal 'plain-songy', flavour is almost invariably introduced. Plain-song is in fact a sort of signature-music for religion on the stage.

And thirdly, from an aesthetic angle, the beauty of harmony and counterpoint is never more apparent than when it is set against a background of unison melody. To 'burst into' a four-part setting of *Magnificat* after the plain-chant of the Psalms, or to do an elaborate Offertory anthem after the plain-song Nicene Creed, is to establish a light and shade in the music of worship which enhances the value of each and gives a much needed variety to the total service of worship.

Having noted this value of unison singing in cathedral services, let us return for an instant to the parish church. The chief duty of the choir here is to lead congregational singing. Would not this duty be more effectively discharged if parish choirs sang far more in unison? The people will of necessity sing in unison. But to be led in this enterprise by singers who cling rigidly to four-part harmony throughout is not really very helpful. It is possible that the singing of Responses and of the Psalms in unison by the choir would far more successfully encourage the people, especially the men, to join in than is usually the case. The aim of corporate worship would thus be better served. It may be added that all Responses become more vital if sung in unison without organ accompaniment.

# V

# THE MATERIALS OF WORSHIP (3)

## Ceremonial

IF words and music are needed as the materials of worship so also is the use of things and objects, and consequently of the bodily actions necessary for their use. A system of ceremonial quite inevitably sprung up in a community for whom the Lord had prescribed the use of water, and of bread and wine, in public worship. Yet it is often taken for granted that while the religion of the old covenant made great use of ceremonial, the religion of the new covenant is, spiritually, an improvement in that it dispenses with it or should try to dispense with it. Christianity, it is held, is unlike Judaism in that it is 'unceremonial', but like it in its spiritual teaching. But really it is the reverse which is true: Christianity is like Judaism in that it has an outward polity in its ministry, sacrifice, ordered liturgy and ceremonial, fast and festival and so on, but in its doctrine and beliefs it exhibits enormous divergence. A popular view of Christian worship is that it is an assembly of men and women whose aim is to be further instructed in moral conduct, both by the reading of the Bible and the exhortation of the preacher. The rest of the service, hymns, prayers, etc., has value in so far as it reinforces the message of the lectern and the pulpit. Such an assembly, while it could not totally avoid the use of material things and movements, has plainly no need for any ceremonial in the classic sense of the word.

But the Christian view is that a congregation is an assembly of sinners who come together in order to approach God through the one availing sacrifice for sins. The Scriptures and the sermon are intended to assist this covenanted approach to God. Prayers are offered not as oblique exhortations to man, not primarily to edify man, but as real requests which must at all costs be made known unto God: hymns and praises are sung, not to convey moral lessons, or to produce an atmosphere, but because praise is God's due, something we owe. And because the one thing which makes worship possible and efficacious is the sacrifice which Christ once offered in the flesh to the Father, and offered not only with His spirit and mind but also with His body, therefore our own participation in that sacrifice must likewise involve our total human nature; spirit, mind and body. Was it not Archbishop William Temple who said, 'Christianity is the least spiritual of all religions'? By which he may have meant that Christianity refuses to isolate the spirit of man from his mind or body, but proclaims the redemption of all. Speaking of Quakers, Archbishop Alexander said:

'They would have no bells, no liturgy, no Sabbath, no stately Minster. For all the spiritual life is one Sabbath, holy to the Lord; and the Spirit himself maketh intercession for us with groanings that cannot be uttered; and God prefers before all temples the upright heart and pure. Sublimely true. Yet we happen to have bodies as well as souls, imagination as well as reason; and we do not happen to be angels or spirits just yet.'[1]

It is for this reason that Christian worship from the beginning involved more than listening and speaking, more than silent, motionless contemplation, more than movements of the heart. It included doing things and using things; postures, gestures, movement from place to place. Ceremonial is the contribution of the body to the offering of the total man. You cannot really avoid using the body in any communal act of worship. You cannot for purposes of worship contract out of the material conditions in which you live, even if it were

[1] *The Great Question*, Wm. Alexander (Kegan Paul, Trench & Co.).

desirable to do so. You cannot demand with reason conditions of worship which are 'purely spiritual'. Even the Quaker must use the organs of speech and hearing. To employ also those of sight, smell and touch; to use arms and legs; all this adds no new principle, except it be the principle of 'wholeness'; the use of your entire being in the worship of the Creator. Worship is giving to God what belongs to Him: all our body, as well as mind and spirit are His.

Ceremonial has two kinds of value. There is the value in using your own body in worship and the value of witnessing others using theirs in a representative capacity. To bow the head before the altar on entering church is not merely to make a public profession of your faith in 'the continual remembrance of the sacrifice of the death of Christ' there set forth: the act of bodily bowing actually deepens your faith and reverence if your general intention is to honour God. To leave your place and walk up to the altar to receive the Holy Sacrament is to increase the urgent sense of needing what God alone gives, and of depending on what God does on His own initiative for our salvation. Imperceptibly every act of blessing yourself with the sign of the cross recalls the signing with the cross in baptism and, however faintly, strengthens your determination to continue a 'faithful soldier and servant'.

So much for 'personal' ceremonial of which a great deal is optional and 'may be used or left as every man's devotion serveth, without blame'.[2] There is also the ceremonial of the officiating minister and his assistants, in the choir and sanctuary. For the most part the people are not called upon to share actively in this: but it is good that individuals should be alert to it and learn to identify themselves with it interiorly, for much of it is performed on their behalf in a representative capacity. Such ceremonial varies in complexity in different places. Though it is not possible, or perhaps desirable, to follow closely every ceremonial act, yet the general

[2] 'Certain Notes' in the 1549 Prayer Book.

sense of each is such that it can become a focus of devotion; it can both interpret the meaning of the liturgy to the individual and also be a vehicle of the individual's adoration towards God: being witnessed by all it can also intensify the sense of worship as a communal act.

Perhaps this needs further elaboration. Those who regularly read the Scriptures and meditate upon them are familiar with this experience: how the reading of a well-pondered passage (such as the parable of the Prodigal Son) will almost instantly organize into a coherent whole the scattered thoughts and separate impressions of many years, knitting them into a single, fervent movement of penitence, or love and gratitude to God. The words thus become either a message to the soul, curiously compact and vivid, or they may become the vehicle of the soul's movement towards God. The familiar words have become a focus. In a similar way a ceremony, familiar since youth or childhood, can perform this all but instantaneous organizing function and call out an immediate response from the soul. The sight of the clergy and their assistants 'humbly kneeling upon their knees' before the altar during the confession can speak to the soul like the words 'he began to be in want' and help to bring to a fine point the worshipper's penitence and contrition. 'And one cried unto another and said Holy, holy, holy is the Lord of hosts: the whole earth is full of his glory.' Words such as these can muster in a flash, into the forefront of the mind and affections, all that a man has ever learned of God's awful sublimity and the plain duty of adoring Him: so can the sight of the incense smoke at the Offertory as it floats upwards, hovering above the oblation. Both the ear and the eye are thus valid and complementary channels, leading to worship with the spirit and with the understanding: bringing both individuals and congregation through a common focus to a common experience of devotion.

Most ceremonial takes its origin from practical necessity. In time, however, it acquires a value supplementary to this. In the institution of the Eucharist it is said that our Lord 'took bread': physically this was a necessity for the accomplishment of His purpose, but the resulting ceremonies of the Offertory, which in the varying rites of Christendom have clothed this action, have acquired a value over and above their plain necessity. As has just been seen, they speak to the individual soul and their employment serves to weld together the intentions of the worshipping community and to make of them a common purpose. The use of lamps and lighted candles took its origin in the physical need for light in a dark place. Though they may still at times perform this function, their use is continued for other purposes. In his sketch of Bishop King of Lincoln, Scott-Holland records an incident[3] in which the Bishop was instructing a shepherd in a village in the Wolds:

> 'He loved one of them, who had slowly learned that the candles on the altar were lighted in broad daylight, because they had no utilitarian purpose. They were not there to give light but to bear witness. "Eh! Then yours is a Yon-side religion, I see, Sir." It appeals, he meant, to something beyond this world.'

Similarly a church-building originated in the need for worshippers to be guarded from prying eyes and protected from inclement weather. It still performs this function, but a churchman sees in his parish church more than a practical expedient, or a concession to human bodily frailty. His church is the place of Baptism where sinful souls are washed, sanctified and made inheritors of the kingdom of heaven. In it the Holy Eucharist is offered in which man gives himself to God in Christ, and God gives Himself to man; in which man draws near with angels and archangels and all the company of heaven; in which he has an earnest, even during his earthly probation, of the glorious destiny to which he is called hereafter. Is it not surprising therefore if, of the construction of stone or wood or bricks called his parish church,

[3] *A Bundle of Memories*, Henry Scott-Holland, p. 61 (Wells, Gardner & Darton, 1915).

he says in the words of Jacob: 'This is none other but the house of God and this is the gate of heaven'? What starts as a practical convenience becomes the earthly symbol of the heavenly Jerusalem. This gives horizon and depth to public worship. This is why he seeks to beautify his church and to lavish money upon its adornment, as a bridegroom does for his bride. This is why he wishes every corner of it to witness to the holiness of God, and to make the last words of v. 9 in Ps. 29 come true: 'In his temple every thing saith, Glory.'

Church ceremonial is eloquent of tradition. The fact that our salvation and our faith are 'traditional', i.e. handed down to us from a divine source within time, must never be forgotten. The modern revolt against tradition, and the increasing belief that each age of men is sufficient unto itself, having no need of what earlier ages can give, has seeped into the imagination even of Christians and affected their outlook profoundly. The sense of the Gospel as something given, of a new covenant once and for all signed and sealed by the Blood of Christ on Golgotha, the sense of the Christian ministry and the Church itself as things which we can only receive and not make for ourselves, needs strengthening in the minds and hearts of worshippers. The modern Christian must be linked in every way with Jesus who came in the flesh and with His mighty acts in time and space in Galilee and Jerusalem. Everything which can impress his imagination with the sense of the handing down and passing on through the ages of this great salvation is of value. 'I received of the Lord that which also I delivered unto you,' said S. Paul. The sense of Christian faith and worship as thus an inheritance which has come down through the years must be impressed upon the worshipper's mind, and conveyed through every possible channel to his being. A traditional ceremonial in the ordering of public worship is one powerful means of effecting this. While the contemporary age should no doubt, though modestly, contribute, and add, to this tradition, its special value lies precisely in its antiquity and in the fact that it is received from earlier ages.

It is often thought that this interest in the inheritance of the past reveals merely a sort of nostalgic romanticism, betraying a flight from the contemporary world, a retreat from present-day reality. Archbishop Davidson used often to maintain[4] that the ceremonial revival in nineteenth-century England came about 'under the influence of Walter Scott "with no necessary doctrinal purpose",' and was wont to cite Dean Stanley as an authority for this view. It is, of course, not impossible that the Waverley novels may have engendered a more benevolent view of the Middle Ages in the imaginations of a number of people. This may well have disposed such to take a more favourable interest in a religious movement which recalled the Church of England to its pre-Reformation past. But to say this is not quite the same as declaring 'that the real author of the Oxford Movement was Sir Walter Scott' as Stanley seems to have done. The Oxford Movement was a recovery of belief in the Church as a visible, authoritative society with a ministry derived from Christ Himself. It had little to say about the pageantry of the Middle Ages, being far more occupied with the teaching and discipline of the Fathers. But as the message of the Tractarians became absorbed by the parochial clergy and their flocks, a recovery of ceremonial usage in time made its appearance. A renewed sense of the continuity of the living society of the Church through the ages demanded a visible expression in outward liturgical forms; while the new stress laid upon ecclesiastical authority led men to take seriously such ceremonial rubrics in the Prayer Book as had hitherto been disregarded. Doctrine and authority were the roots from which ceremonial revived: it had little to do with antiquarian aestheticism. Ceremonial tradition sprang inevitably to new life under the influence of an awakened sense of doctrinal tradition. Ceremonial in worship is in fact a recognition through visible acts and ornaments of the great high road which leads down to the contemporary scene from Galilee and Jerusalem, through

[4] *Randall Davidson*, G. K. A. Bell (Oxford University Press), Vol. I, pp. 124, 464.

## THE MATERIALS OF WORSHIP 57

Antioch, Athens, Patmos, Rome, through the middle ages, and the Reformation era, and Victorian England. The vesture of ministers, the fragrant smoke of the censer, the solemn movements to and fro, the flickering lights, the laying on of hands, the altar rails, the clear and distinct reading of God's Word—all these things are as milestones on the great road, and help to assure the worshipper that his faith is no hotchpotch of contemporary notions but the authentic inheritance from the Heir who was slain and cast out of the vineyard but who returned the third day and said to His apostles: 'As the Father sent me, even so send I you.'

Ceremonial thus has a twofold social function: it is both a link between contemporary worshippers all over the present world, and a link between congregations of all ages, leading back to those moments in this visible world when our salvation was given by God incarnate.

If ceremonial is to play a healthy part in the Church's worship it must have an authoritative basis. Both rite and ceremony must have the quality of given-ness and not be the mere fruit of self-will or sentimental fashion. Amid the religious changes in the sixteenth century the Church of England clung to a policy of re-formation and repudiated revolution. It therefore insisted upon the retention of at least a minimum of traditional ceremonial, and upon the Church's 'power to decree Rites or Ceremonies'. It clung to this twofold principle with dogged tenacity in spite of a strong opposition lasting almost a century and a half. What went on in churches at service time must be the 'rites and ceremonies of *the Church* according to *the use* of the Church of England' as the title page of the Prayer Book made clear. Article 34 laid it down that 'Whosoever through his private judgement willingly and purposely doth openly break the traditions and ceremonies of the Church, which be not repugnant to the Word of God, and be ordained and approved by common authority, ought to be rebuked openly, as he that offendeth against the common order of the Church, and hurteth the authority of the Magistrate and woundeth the conscience of the weak brethren.' The Preface entitled 'Of Ceremonies' described them as being deliberately retained 'as well for a decent order in the Church . . . as because they pertain to edification,' while it insisted that the very antiquity of ceremonies was one reason for their value and deprecated 'innovations and new-fangleness'. Nevertheless, the maintenance of even a very jejune standard required much determination and firmness through many generations.

During the past hundred years it has become apparent that the hard Puritan opposition to ceremonial has to a great extent disintegrated, and this period (as has been noted above) has seen a widespread movement for the recovery of more outward observance than the authorities at the Reformation era thought prudent or even desirable. This movement has not been confined to the Church of England, but has emerged also to some extent in the Free Churches.

Despite this, ceremonial is frequently employed to an extent which is not always appreciated by the laity. Such distaste is by no means usually due to mistrust of ceremonial on grounds of principle. It is sometimes due to the recovery of elaborate ceremonial having been hasty and revolutionary.

People are nearly always, and rightly, conservative in all that concerns the sanctuary. A complete sweeping away of familiar landmarks and the substitution of a new and almost unintelligible series of ornaments and ceremonies, however authentic, engenders a sense of outrage which goes very deep, and may have long-term and serious spiritual results. At the best it creates an inward disorder, analogous to indigestion, which is only less harmful than the sense of outrage. However meagre and unprincipled was the previous regime, it had been for the people their tradition, their link back through the ages with their worshipping forefathers. To see this destroyed overnight cannot but be harmful to the soul. Just because ceremonies are so important, they cannot take root without the most careful and diligent planting: they are to be handled delicately, and with reverent care and sympathy. The recovery of ceremonial will totally fail in its great mission of conveying a sense of continuity and tradition if it is carried out like the putting on of a new play at the theatre. That is one reason why ceremonial recovery is sometimes ineffectual.

Another is when a system of ceremonial which has grown up in another part of the world, round a different rite, is transplanted and used with the Prayer Book liturgy. Such a project is usually contrary to the authority of the Prayer Book. Further there is a psychological incongruity between the two which, though easy to discern, is hard to analyse. Just as Mozart's operas, given in English, are apt to be strangely disappointing, so Cranmer's English clothed in a modern Roman ceremonial dress does not 'come off'. The two have grown up in wholly different *milieux* and will not fuse. You always have the impression that the ceremonial is merely added and stuck on from the outside, for inwardly there is little affinity between the two. The Prayer Book rises out of an English past, and demands a ceremonial expression of similar origin and history. It is to this English past that the Ornaments Rubric[5] points us when ceremonial recovery is desired: since that Rubric was devised, there has been a further four hundred years of tradition (by no means always negative) which deserves careful and sympathetic study. To assume that no respectable or valuable ceremonial has grown up in England since the Church revised its rite in the sixteenth and seventeenth centuries is to fall into a very common error.

Wherever people really believe in something, and are not uneasy or self-conscious in their belief, ritual and ceremonial inevitably plays an important part in their lives. There is something inherent in our nature which demands an outlet in ritual speech or song and in ceremonial movement and action. Life was once full of it at the civic, the social and the family level. But in recent years it has been ebbing away

---

[5] This is the Rubric printed immediately before the Order for Morning Prayer. It has been the subject of lengthy controversy. It is assumed here that the second half of the Rubric at least permits, where desirable, the use of furniture, vesture and other liturgical objects in use on the eve of the appearance of the first Prayer Book of 1549, when such use is not incompatible with the liturgy of the Prayer Book and its doctrinal standards.

and the public and private life of man is lived increasingly on a dim grey utilitarian plain; undifferentiated by the hills of festival and solemn rejoicing, or the valleys of mourning and humiliation. It was these hills and valleys which were primarily the occasions of ritual and ceremonial. Yet man's natural hunger for these still finds its outlet: freemasonry and other friendly societies provide opportunity for their initiates, while community-singing at football matches and other occasions is perhaps the nearest thing we have to social, ecstatic utterance. But for the most part modern man is compelled to live most of his life without that ritual and ceremonial rhythm which was once so dear to him and for which he still has an aching need. You have only to watch the faces of the crowd witnessing the change of Guard at Buckingham Palace, or the Trooping of the Colour, to know how native to the human soul is the love of ceremonial and colour. Usurping governments know this well and they are lavish in their expenditure of trouble and money in providing grand ceremonial occasions both for their votaries, and for the youth of the countries whom they seek to win to their allegiance. All the more then should it be the care of the Christian Church to see that this instinct is carefully provided for in its public worship, and not to keep up any pretence of being spiritually superior to so essential a demand of humanity.

# VI

# THE BOOK OF COMMON PRAYER

HAVING now reviewed in a general way the nature of public worship and examined some of the principles involved, we pass to a consideration of public worship as envisaged and ordered in the Book of Common Prayer: and so that the scheme of that book shall be better understood, a brief account of its origin here follows, together with an attempt to emphasize the main intentions and desires of its compilers.

*History*

It was in 1549 that the first English Book of Common Prayer came into use. It involved an immense change in the way English people worshipped. Why was change thought necessary? During the Middle Ages the services had been almost entirely in Latin, a language which had gradually become unintelligible except to a minority. In a broad way the people knew what was going on in church because they could follow the ceremonial with their eyes. They could join in the service at least in spirit to some extent: they could probably sing parts of it. But they could not follow the priest's prayers or make his words their own because of the language difficulty. The service was conducted by the priest and responses were made by the clerks who assisted him. The congregation were little more than interested spectators, however devout.

In earlier days the language of the service had been familiar. The people then could, and were encouraged, to take their full share, in heart and voice; but by the end of the Middle Ages this situation had completely altered and the congregation had all but lost its active share in the offering of public worship. Those who could read had primers and could use individually some of the devotional material they contained while the services were going on; but the actual words of the liturgy and the readings from the Bible could not be followed or understood. Further, though the principal service was the Mass or the Holy Communion, no one except the priest normally received the Sacrament, nor were the people encouraged to do so. This again was a decline from earlier usage when the Sunday Mass had been the occasion for general communion.

Even had they understood the language of the services the people would have found their character different from earlier days. Then, the services had contained far more of the Bible with larger and more varied readings and a far more thorough use of the psalms, even at the Eucharist: but both readings and psalms had been very drastically reduced. Preaching also had become infrequent. Though the people knew some of the outlines of Christian teaching and belief, they were not constantly being refreshed and deepened in their faith. They learned a certain amount from witnessing the ceremonies of the liturgy. But even these had become complicated and had lost their earlier and simpler outlines.

There was one part of the Sunday morning service into which the congregation could unreservedly enter. It was called the Bidding of the Bedes and was done in English. It consisted of a detailed intercession for the needs of daily life, containing prayers for the clergy, for the King and the nobility, the prosperity of the realm, and also for the needs of ordinary people in the parish, naming their various callings, and foreseeing their necessities. This form of prayer survives till this day under the title of the Bidding Prayer. It has always been popular and its ethos strongly pervades the Prayer Book in what has been called 'the homely, practical, incarnational temper of English piety, with its close and determined association of religion with all the events and anxieties of daily life'.

Such then, in the most general outline, was the character of English public worship on the eve of the Reformation. An American Roman Catholic priest, Father Paul Bussard, makes this comment:[1] 'In the sixteenth century the Mass itself had become the centre of a lush growth of credulity which on many occasions did not escape deserving the name of superstition.' Dr. Leighton Pullan, an Anglican divine, wrote: 'The *heart* of medieval English religion was not superstition. It was devotion to our Lord Jesus Christ in His Passion. But it was enfeebled by superstition and it was right to purge that superstition.'

The need for this purge was not confined to England, nor was the determination to do so a mere piece of English insularity. As far north as Sweden, liturgical reform under Olaus Petri began in 1529, while in the remote territory of Finland, Michael Agricola, Bishop of Abo, brought out a liturgy in the Finnish tongue in the very year of our own first Prayer Book. In Germany, reform began earlier, under Luther, and issued in a multitude of *Kirchenordnungen* or schemes for church services together with catechisms containing liturgical material. On the Rhine, Hermann von Wied, Prince Archbishop of Cologne, inaugurated important changes in worship, some of which influenced our own Prayer Book, while Zurich and Geneva likewise provided themselves with new forms of public prayer. Less radical than most of these is the book known as Quignon's Breviary. Clement VII, anxious to clear away some of the difficulties which handicapped the clergy in their duty of reading the daily service, asked Cardinal Francis de Quinonez, a Spanish Franciscan, to revise the Breviary. This was done in a very thorough manner. Of his book, which appeared in 1535, no fewer than one hundred editions were printed in the next thirty-three years. Similar attempts at reform were made in different parts of France, though without Quignon's success. They are evidence of the universal desire for liturgical reform even

---

[1] *The Vernacular Missal in Religious Education,* by Paul Bussard (The Catholic University of America, Washington, D.C., 1937), p. 5.

in countries which remained loyal to the papacy. This desire Rome itself recognized as legitimate, in the revision of its own official service books by the Council of Trent. It is in this setting and not merely in a domestic setting that we must view the production of the first English Book of Common Prayer.

What changes did this Prayer Book bring about in church services? First of all, the English tongue was substituted for the Latin. The reformers thus reintroduced a principle of worship which had been known in earlier days. The earliest liturgy used at Rome was in Greek. At the end of the fourth century the Latin language was substituted because Greek was no longer the ordinary spoken language. At a later date, when S. Cyril, the Apostle of the Slavs, introduced (about A.D. 865) services in Slavonic he was rebuked by Rome. But opening a Psalter he read out: '"Let everything that hath breath praise the Lord." If everything that hath breath is to praise the Lord,' he went on, 'why, my fathers, do you forbid us to perform the Mass in the Slavonic tongue?' We are told his arguments were successful and he was allowed to continue the use of the vernacular. The English reformers followed Cyril's example. Their hope was that not only would people thus know what was going on in church, but that they would use the very words of the service as the vehicle of their individual prayer and praise. Thus, in the preface attached to the English Litany on its first appearance in 1544 it was said:

> And such among the people as have books and can read may read them quietly and softly to themselves; and such as cannot read, let them quietly and attentively give audience in time of the said prayer, having their minds erect to Almighty God and devoutly praying in their hearts the same petitions which do enter in at their ears so that with one sound of the heart and with one accord God may be glorified in his Church.

The reformers' aim was that the congregation should pray the liturgy and not be content merely to pray their private prayers while the liturgy was recited by the priest and clerks. This aim could only have been attained if service books could be produced more or less cheaply and in sufficient numbers:

the comparatively recent invention of printing made this possible. The aim would similarly have failed had not a roughly uniform version of the English language by now established itself in nearly every part of the country, after its long period of slow development. Providence indeed favoured the reformers. It might be said with some truth that in the sphere of public worship the Reformation in England was a 're-discovery of the congregation'. In the later Middle Ages the people had almost no function in worship except as pious witnesses. Such was a grave decline from the community-action of earlier Christian worship and the reformers were determined to remedy it.

The change of language was a first step, but this was part of an even more fundamental change—the new note of edification. To be edified as a worshipper means to be supplied with material which will stimulate worship. In the Middle Ages the element of edification was to be found in the ceremonies of the church, and in the beauty of architecture and the other visible accessories of worship: but all this edified mainly the non-rational part of a man. It tended to leave his understanding without resources. Words were not used for edification, for they were uttered hurriedly and in a tongue unknown. The reformers on the other hand tended to place all their confidence in words as the source of edification, and to neglect that large and valuable area of human personality which is not rational. Edification of the worshipper by the words of Holy Scripture, the words of the preacher and the words of liturgical exhortations formed a major part of their plan. Almost no service in the Prayer Book is without its Exhortation, a device already used in the older liturgies of Gaul and Spain, but one which the reformers borrowed on perhaps too lavish a scale. Its aim is to stir the heart and mind and will of the congregation to embark upon the business of worship with a zeal inflamed by knowledge. The provision of the novelty of a weekly sermon was a step in the same direction, though its scope was somewhat wider than the Exhortation.

But it was upon Holy Scripture itself that the reformers most relied in their aim of edifying men as true worshippers. The Biblical element in popular worship was not an innovation but a re-discovery. It had never vanished though it had become obscured. The reformers restored an element which had been the foundation of early Christian worship. They believed that a return to the Bible in worship would build up a worshipping community, informed, rational and devout. As the preface to the first Prayer Book puts it, the Bible must be used so 'that the people (by daily hearing of Holy Scripture read in the Church) might continually profit more and more in the knowledge of God and be the more inflamed with the love of his true religion'.

To further this aim the reformers provided for popular use services in addition to the Eucharist, consisting almost wholly of the recitation of the Psalms and readings from the Bible. Such worship had always been offered by the Church and was known as the Divine Office. But for hundreds of years this type of prayer had been confined to the clergy, though originally it had been otherwise. In order to bring such services within reach of the laity their daily number was reduced from eight to two and their character greatly simplified. It was simplified mainly with the intention of securing a continuous reading of the Bible and Psalter, not interrupted by a throng of festivals each with special psalms and lessons; it followed in fact the lines of Cardinal Quinonez's Breviary to which reference has already been made.

These services, called Mattins and Evensong, became eventually very popular, but they were not intended by the reformers to occupy that central place in Anglican Sunday worship which they in fact eventually did. The reformers wished to retain the Holy Communion as the climax of at least Sunday worship.[2] This climax was to be led up to by Mattins and the Litany and followed up later by Evensong: but this plan did not succeed. As previously mentioned, in the later Middle Ages Mass was celebrated normally without

[2] See J. Wordsworth, *The Holy Communion*, p. 147.

communicants other than the priest, except at Easter. The reformers believed that Mass without communicants was an abuse and that communion once a year was not enough. In the hope of increasing the occasions of communion it was decreed that unless a certain number of communicants came forward there should be no celebration of the Eucharist. The medieval habit of only annual communion was, however, stronger than the reformers hoped and so it came about that the Holy Communion was only infrequently celebrated. The Sunday morning service therefore tended to settle down as Mattins, Litany and the first part of the Communion service; though this does not seem to have been the reformers' desire. The re-discovery of the congregation, its ingathering into a conscious community act of worship, its edification by preaching, the constant use of the Scriptures, and the general return to the ways of the Church before its great division and separation into east and west—these were some of the principal aims of the reformers.

But there was at least one other. Troubles on the Continent caused a number of foreign theologians of the reformed school to seek refuge on our hospitable shore. These men came from centres where the Reformation had found more radical expression both in doctrine and methods of worship than was known in England. Inevitably they gained a following in this country and established a more revolutionary party in ecclesiastical circles. This party was not satisfied with the comparatively conservative reforms of the first Prayer Book of 1549. They wanted something more drastic, something more in accord with the Protestant doctrines of Geneva. Archbishop Cranmer was far from being in complete agreement with this school of extremists, yet he did not wish totally to exclude their influence from English Church life. In fact he invited some of them to criticize the Prayer Book and to set forth their views. On the other hand, Cranmer did not wish to alienate the conservative party which, while ready to break with Rome, was yet tenacious of traditional practice and belief. It seemed plain to the Archbishop that, if these two parties were to be able to live and worship together in the Church of England, some further revision of the Prayer Book must take place. This new edition of the Prayer Book appeared in 1552. Its aim was 'to reassure the English Catholics without readmitting the Pope and to keep open the road to union with the moderate Continental Protestants'.

This immediate purpose was not achieved, for it was not found possible to line up Continental Protestantism with the conservative spirit of English reform. The Book of 1552 was thus a failure; and indeed was scarcely used at all. Nevertheless, its subsequent revisions under Queen Elizabeth I, James I and Charles II, which produced the book we have to-day, have succeeded in realizing Cranmer's inclusive policy in a long-term fashion. A prominent characteristic of the Prayer Book is what its friends would call eirenic and its enemies compromise. It contains a liturgy which men of both Catholic and Evangelical sympathies can and do conscientiously use. Though it was at one stage designed to meet a definite historical crisis and though it failed to do that satisfactorily, it has nevertheless in the long run, with few alterations, succeeded in this direction perhaps beyond the reformers' most sanguine hopes. I cannot illustrate this better than by quoting from Miss Evelyn Underhill:

> The puzzled student of Anglicanism can find within its borders, and using its liturgic books, an almost complete Evangelicalism: grave, Biblical, prophetic, devoted, based on the preaching and hearing of the Word, suspicious of ceremonial acts and sensible signs, emphasizing the personal relation of the soul to God, greatly concerned with man, his needs, problems and duties, and hardly distinguishable in temper from the unstylized public worship of the Nonconformist sects. But he can also find, using the same books and obedient to the same authorities, a sacramental, objective, and theocentric worship; emphasizing the holiness, authority, and total action of the Church, her call to adoration and vocation of sacrifice, reverencing her traditions and her saints, using all the resources of symbolic expression.[3]

[3] *Worship*, by Evelyn Underhill (Nisbet, 1936), p. 323.

In short, the hopes and aims of the reformers when launching the Prayer Book in the sixteenth century were not in vain.

*Character*

So much for the genesis of the Prayer Book and the principal aims of its compilers. Much more could be said about this and much general description given of the main characteristics of the services which the book provides, but there is one such characteristic which needs for various reasons to be described at some length.

An increasing element in modern religious life is the desire of many institutions, societies, vocational groups, and so on to assemble in force at the parish church on some anniversary or other occasion for a special service. The initiative is probably taken by a few members who are keen churchmen, but they bring with them to the service many who scarcely ever enter a church on any other occasion and whose knowledge of the Christian faith is meagre and limited. This widespread desire to come to church as a community is a very remarkable and welcome movement, even if at times it is hard to estimate what it portends.

On such occasions the service is frequently not in accordance with the Prayer Book but follows some order drawn up locally in which the history, needs, and aims of the society in question are prominently reflected in its hymns, exhortations, prayers and Bible readings. Interest is naturally aroused, and many perhaps hitherto unfamiliar with public worship take a new view of the value of Church services. Some of these accordingly start attending church sporadically on their own, but when they do so they may find that an 'ordinary' church service is not so interesting to them as the 'special' service which first quickened their interest. It lacks, they feel, the human touch, and does not convey any special message. They may wonder why this is so and what it is in the 'ordinary' service which is so different from the 'special' service. They have indeed been confronted with the fact that the Prayer Book does not provide a series of services, each complete in itself, isolated from other services, and able to stand alone. There are many Christian bodies whose acts of worship are like this, complete in themselves, connected with past and future only by being numerically one of a series of similar acts in a given place. The form used on any one occasion has no essential dependence upon the form used on the preceding occasion, or upon the next. It stands alone and is intended to be the best form of worship possible in that congregation at that particular moment in the history of the world.

But this is not the case in Anglican worship according to the Prayer Book. There a church service, as regards its content and form, is both complete and incomplete: it is possible to view it as distinct from all other past and future services, and yet equally as dependent on those preceding it and those following it. There, individual services are like cells in an organism, each one complete and distinct in itself, yet forming an organic unity with other cells, in which they achieve a total significance and value greater than the value of the separate cells added together.

This inter-dependence of Prayer Book services on one another, so that, while each is complete from one aspect, it is yet incomplete from another, can be illustrated in three ways.

First: it was said earlier in the chapter that the compilers of the Prayer Book intended Mattins and Evensong, among other things, to be a means by which 'the people (by daily hearing of Holy Scripture read in the church) might continually profit more and more in the knowledge of God'. The reading of most of the Bible right through, connectedly, in course, had been a feature of the pre-medieval Church, but gradually this practice of continuous reading had broken down because of the endless interruptions caused by the growth of festivals and saints' days each requiring special readings. The more ancient practice was restored in the Prayer Book, and measures were taken to prevent its interruption by special readings except on rare occasions. Though these occasions have tended to increase, the modern practice in the Anglican Church is still to adhere more or less strictly to the principle of continuous reading of the books in the Bible and at each service the lessons follow on from the last.

As daily attendance at Mattins and Evensong by the laity is no longer envisaged as likely (though the Reformers had more sanguine hopes) the Revised Prayer Book has met the modern situation in a practical way. It provides for two courses or cycles of Bible lessons, a Sunday course and a weekday course. Those who attend only upon Sundays still enjoy a more or less connected course of Bible reading, each Sunday's lessons roughly following on from those of the previous Sunday. The weekday course, now used mainly by the clergy, is similarly, though more strictly, constructed. While the whole Bible is, with some exception, read through once a year (the New Testament being read through twice), the Psalms of David are recited once a month (almost) on weekdays and (roughly) twice a year on Sundays.

This means that at Mattins or Evensong, on some occasion not a festival, the particular lesson read is not read because it seems to the clergyman to be specially appropriate or specially edifying. It is read because it is a part of that book in the Bible whose turn for being read has come round. The fact that the, say, fifth chapter is read to-day is because the fourth was read yesterday: the first chapter was read four days ago because the Church thinks it fit to read nearly the whole of the Bible and the turn of that book then fell due. It is the same with the psalms. In this way the services of Mattins and Evensong depend upon one another and must be viewed not as isolated acts of worship each with specially selected material considered appropriate to the occasion.

The Bible is never fully appreciated in all its parts by any one generation of men: each generation has its preferences and even its aversions, which are not always shared by the generation which succeeds it. So it comes about that on a given day impulse brings some infrequent worshipper to church where he hears a lesson which is barely intelligible to him: what *is* intelligible is uncongenial. He does not reflect that, had he been more faithful in his duty of worship, he would have heard earlier passages in the book which would have prepared him for the lesson he then found unintelligible and filled it with meaning, or that if regularly present he might have received instruction which would have mitigated the offence given to his sense of fitness. Instead he regards the service in question as an isolated event in which every word in psalm or lesson should be immediately clear to him and wholly edifying (as in a 'special' service).

But it is hardly possible to provide a fixed liturgy for Christian worship in which each and every service is wholly intelligible and edifying to any chance attender, and which at the same time bears balanced witness to the whole Christian faith. If a liturgy is to be the authentic voice of the Church in adoration of the true God, using the entire Scriptures as the materials of its worship, it is bound to include a number of services which seem less edifying than others, and which cannot equally illuminate or uplift everyone who happens to be present. It must in fact provide for a continuity in worship in which the services 'hang together' and for which regularity in attendance is essential if the scheme is to yield up its true value.

It may well be necessary, in these days of widespread unbelief and unfamiliarity with the Gospel, to compile a series of services, additional to the Liturgy, in which the aim would be rather instruction and exercise in the art of worshipping, designed to lead on to a full participation in the Liturgy itself. But it is extremely short-sighted to pare away the Prayer Book services till they reach some level of supposed congruity with prevailing ignorance, prejudice or misunderstanding. When such a project is adopted it means in practice a narrow censorship of the Scriptures, which in turn reduces the quantity of the Bible read to a range perhaps less wide even than in the Middle Ages. Further, it is apt to confine the Scripture readings to sections which appear to exhort man to make greater efforts after moral welfare. The continuous and connected use of the Scriptures in public worship is thus the first reason for the close dependence of some of the services upon one another.

A second way in which the separate services provided for in the Prayer Book are yet dependent upon one another, and do not stand alone, can be seen in the operation of the Liturgical Year. Taken by itself, the office of Mattins or Evensong on any day seems deliberately planned in its structure to be a memorial of our Redemption. Consider this statement in the instance, say, of Mattins on the first Sunday in Advent. After the introductory part, the psalms proper to the day (as given in the Revised Prayer Book) are sung. They are Psalms 1 and 7. Psalm 1 utters the aspiration of unredeemed humanity for a perfect sonship of God, acknowledging that apart from this sonship, man must perish. Psalm 7 emphasizes the inevitability of God's judgment upon man as a sinner. The first lesson (Isa. 1.1-20) goes deeper, uncovering the thoughts and activities of man at his best and showing even his worship to be corrupt; it ends with the divine call to repentance and with the promise of forgiveness. At this point, as we pass from the Old Testament to the New, a hymn of praise is sung in honour of the promise of God, whether *Te Deum Laudamus* or *Benedicite*. Then the second lesson is read (John 3.1-21) in which Christ proclaims the new birth into the Kingdom of God, brought about by the Father's gift of His only begotten Son. This in turn gives way to the hymn *Benedictus*, in which we view the future through the prophetic eyes of Zacharias, and see all that flows from the 'mighty salvation' wrought by Christ as bringer of forgiveness, light and peace. The act has its conclusion in the collect for Advent Sunday in which we pray that by God's grace we may pass through the Judgement to the resurrection in the 'life immortal'.

In this act of worship we rehearse before God our need of redemption and the means by which He has brought it about: we dispose ourselves to receive the benefit of that redemption and to identify ourselves with the process of salvation set forth stage by stage in psalm and hymn: in lesson and collect. It is a coherent act, moving dramatically and rationally from stage to stage, roughly covering the ground of our faith and hope. As such it can stand by itself.

Yet the picture given of our salvation on this single Sunday is very much in monochrome. It is like a pencil sketch which omits no essential detail, but upon which no colour is laid save the prevalent and sombre hue of judgement. The psalms and lessons bear witness to other elements, to man's capacity for moral indignation, and for delight in the Lord, to God's love, patience and long-suffering, and the Apostles' Creed recites the entire scheme of Redemption, but towering above all is the picture of God as Judge and man as in danger. This picture is true and yet it is not all the truth. God is more than Judge. For this reason, though Mattins on Advent Sunday must needs be recited, and its full implications acknowledged, it cannot be considered 'complete' as an act of Christian worship. To be complete it is dependent on Mattins on Christmas Day when God as Son incarnate is set forth, when the Psalms speak of the Saviour of man coming forth 'as a bridegroom out of his chamber and rejoicing as a giant to run his course'; of how 'mercy and truth are met together: righteousness and peace have kissed each other' because God has become gracious unto His land: when the first lesson takes us back to the people of the Old Covenant who looked forward to the day men would say 'unto us a child is born, unto us a son is given . . . of the increase of his government and peace there shall be no end'; when the second lesson proclaims the fulfilment of this hope as the shepherds 'found Mary, and Joseph, and the babe lying in a manger' This rectifies and gives due proportion to the memorial of God as Judge set before us on Advent Sunday. Yet it is still deficient, for Christmas needs Epiphany and both need Passiontide and Easter, if worship is to be worship of the true God as He has revealed Himself to us.

That is why a fixed liturgy is provided with a Calendar. A Calendar is needed in which the successive stages of our deliverance are set forth at intervals throughout the year, in the light of which the daily worship of God is offered. As each festival or fast comes round the story of our redemption is recited 'with special reference to' the implications of the event or mystery commemorated at that day or season. This ensures that the worship of the Church is 'coloured' successively by all the events in which we profess our faith in the Creeds, and prevents public worship in any place being confined to the influence merely of the truths in which some local president of worship may be specially interested. The services of the Church are thus in due and balanced proportion informed by 'the whole counsel of God'. The story of our redemption is, as it were, 'lived over again' in every single and separate act of worship, and yet in another sense only in the whole series of services throughout a year. Each service may be considered as a complete act in one sense; in another, each service every day is dependent upon all the other services of the year for its completeness.

But besides the dependence of one service upon another, made to some extent necessary by the Liturgical Year and by the continuous reading of Scripture, there is a third way in which they are mutually inter-dependent. Every Sunday and Holy Day in the Prayer Book is provided with a proper Epistle and Gospel, in addition to the prescribed psalms and lessons. This means that on a Sunday or Holy Day the services are to be Mattins (Litany), Holy Communion and Evensong. Some Prayer Book rubrics[4] further reveal at least a hope that on ordinary weekdays celebrations of Holy Communion may be held using the Collect, Epistle, Gospel (and Proper Preface) of the Sunday.

Ideally, then, at least the Liturgy of every day finds its climax in the Eucharist. In this sense the day is as much a unit of worship as is the year or the liturgical season. Mattins (and on some days the Litany) leads up to the Eucharist, by

[4] After the Gospel for the Circumcision of Christ, and before most of the Proper Prefaces in the Holy Communion. Also at the end of *The Order how the rest of Holy Scripture is appointed to be read.*

way of preparation and expectation, while Evensong is thanksgiving for the Holy Sacrifice on which our redemption depends. This is occasionally made doubly clear in the Prayer Book where the second lesson at Mattins is continued as the Epistle or Gospel at the Holy Communion.[5]

So much then for the quality of Prayer Book services as in one way complete as separate acts, but in another way mutually dependent on one another. It is very important to remember for otherwise it is so easy to drop into the habit of regarding any single service as a devotional act which ought to be specially prepared for each occasion of worship, rather than as one necessary passage in a great epic of praise which the Church offers from year to year in praise of the Blessed Trinity.

[5] e.g. on Palm Sunday and Good Friday.

## VII

## EUCHARIST AND SACRIFICE

WE shall soon pass to a consideration of some of the Prayer Book services in detail. It may have surprised some that in the remarks upon the general character of these services in the last chapter so much was said of Mattins and Evensong, and so little of the Holy Communion which is the climax of Christian worship. But this book is intended mainly for those who are not closely associated with Anglican worship and whose contacts with it are chiefly in its non-sacramental aspects. Illustrations of the character of Anglican worship were naturally drawn first from the services which are most familiar to them.

But the Holy Communion is the climax and heart of Christian worship: it stands closest of all to that Divine Mystery of Redemption without which any acceptable worship would be impossible. This centrality of the Holy Communion is well symbolized in the format of the Prayer Book, for the Order of Service for its celebration is printed as nearly as possible in the middle of the book (if the Ordinal and 39 Articles are not reckoned as part of the book, to which they are indeed supplements). Many names for this holy rite have been, and are, current in Christendom. The Prayer Book at present uses two names, the Holy Communion and the Lord's Supper. The first Prayer Book of 1549 made use of the title Mass, a name which is used by Roman Catholics and by the Lutherans of Scandinavia, but which has not found favour with the great majority of Anglicans. Following the example of Dr. Daniel Waterland, an Anglican theologian of the early eighteenth century, we shall mainly employ the name Eucharist which indeed is the custom of the majority of Anglican writers.

## Sacrifice

The Eucharist is fundamentally sacrificial worship and it is with the Prayer Book Communion Service as a sacrificial rite that this chapter is primarily concerned. 'The Lord's Supper,' says the Prayer Book Catechism, 'was ordained for the continual remembrance of the sacrifice of the death of Christ, and of the benefits which we receive thereby.'

The notion of sacrifice in connection with worship is apt either to disgust, or to bewilder, contemporary minds. Sacrifice as a mode of approaching God is thought to be either long dead, except among primitive tribes, or if not, as something which ought to be dead and which could not conceivably find any respectable place in the 'religion of the twentieth century'. It is thought to be so old an institution that it cannot possibly have any truth or relevance for civilized man. This was evidently the difficulty of the late Bernard Shaw who, in his *Adventures of the Black Girl in her Search for God*, says:

> 'We find Paul holding up Christ to the Ephesians as "an offering and a sacrifice to God for a sweet-smelling savour" thereby dragging Christianity back and down to the level of Noah. None of the apostles rose above that level.'

The implication of this outburst seems to be that nothing that Noah believed could still be of importance in the middle years of the first century A.D. and that therefore S. Paul (who seemed to think that it could) may be dismissed as a serious teacher of truth. Shaw did not stop to speculate or enquire what may have been Noah's motive in sacrificing to God, or whether S. Paul's notion of sacrifice was, or was not, identical with Noah's. He merely observed that S. Paul uses the same word as was used in Genesis and, without further examination, concluded that S. Paul, with the rest of the apostles, was unprogressive and obscurantist. He let himself be dazzled by the mere age of the word sacrifice. Many follow his example.

But Shaw's observation at least supports the vital truth that the Bible from first to last never lets you escape from the fact of sacrifice. From Cain and Abel in Genesis to the 'Lamb standing, as though it had been slain' in the Apocalypse, the Bible witnesses to the unceasing pre-occupation of the people of God with sacrifice as the true approach to God in worship. This is as true after the Ascension of Christ as before His' coming. A conception of worship divorced from sacrifice could be neither Biblical nor Christian.

But all this is not to say that Noah's beliefs about sacrifice were identical with S. Paul's, any more than that Moses' conceptions of the moral law were identical with that expounded in the Sermon on the Mount. Christ came, however, not to destroy but to fulfil. Just as He does not abolish the Ten Commandments but reveals heights and depths within them not previously discerned, so He does not abolish the Law of sacrifice but transforms it. Noah was not wrong in his impulse to approach God in his thanksgiving by sacrifice, even though his philosophy of sacrifice may have been gravely defective. Our Lord in speaking of His own death as the outpouring of the 'blood of the new covenant' showed that Noah had at least been groping in the right direction.

A second reason for the repugnance with which men commonly regard sacrifice is the deeply ingrained misconception that the essence of sacrifice is destruction and slaughter.

'The "Man in the street", and many who are more familiar with theology than he, would still, if they were asked to describe a sacrifice, suggest an altar, with a living victim bound upon it, and a priest standing over it with a knife in his uplifted hand. Translated into the language of the Christian sacrifice, that is the conception of Christ offering Himself upon the Altar of the Cross, of sacrifice as equivalent to, and completed in, death.'[1]

[1] *The Fullness of Sacrifice*, by F. C. N. Hicks (Macmillan, 1938), p. 327.

To this picture of action a motive is supplied, namely that the killing of the victim is, as an end in itself, pleasing to God who thereby becomes favourable to the offerer of the sacrifice. Is it going too far to say that such a total picture comes into the imagination of many whenever the words sacrifice or blood occur in the Liturgy or in hymns sung in church?

But, thirdly, even if no difficulty is felt about the sufferings and death of Christ, and they are regarded as part of a perfect life of obedience and loyalty to the Father's will in a world of sinful men and as such, a perfect offering of enduring love; how can this transaction benefit anyone else other than as a salutary example of moral faithfulness? How, by any 'pleading' of this sacrifice, do I claim any moral right to profit by it myself? How can this offering enable me to approach God, since I am still the same person as I was before? If unfit to approach God because of my inner spiritual condition, how does the 'showing forth' of Christ's sacrifice in the solemn rite of the Eucharist enable me to do so?

And fourthly, if the Eucharist is Christ's sacrifice, does this not imply a belief that at every celebration of that rite the whole offering must be done again? And as the essence of sacrifice is thought to reside in the slaying and the dying, does not this imply the belief that Christ is slain over and over again whenever the Eucharist is offered? How can this be reconciled with the teaching of the New Testament about the 'one sacrifice for sins, for ever' offered 'once for all'?

Nothing further need be said about the objection, felt rather than uttered, that worship through sacrifice is irrelevant because the conception and practice are so old. But something must be said about the essential nature of sacrifice and of the place in it which death and blood occupy. Doubtless there have been people who believed that divine beings could be won over by the mere ritual slaughter of animals or men, and who called this rite sacrifice. Similarly there have been others who believed that the gods could be bribed and that this could be brought about by the ritual transfer to them of valuable property in the shape of agricultural produce or farm stock. Such beliefs are, however, but stages in the growth of human understanding of the true meaning of sacrifice. The instinct to worship God in a *costing* manner: the belief that it is wrong and ineffectual to appear empty-handed before Him: these form the impulse which has sustained the practice of sacrifice from the earliest times, together with the hope that through such worship man might be brought near to God and have fellowship with Him. But the interpretation of that impulse, its purification from baser motives and crude hopes, and the evolution of a philosophy of sacrifice with a high ethical content—this process has finally resulted in a doctrine of sacrifice with which the Saviour of mankind has associated Himself in the most solemn and emphatic manner.

In seeking to understand this doctrine it is first of all necessary to avoid thinking of death as the end and final justification of an act of sacrifice, or of blood outpoured as the mere physical result of a violent death. At least with the Jews, death was but an inevitable stage in sacrifice, while blood was not the mere evidence of death and bodily hurt. The blood was regarded as 'the life' of the victim, now released from its corporal limitation and available for a higher purpose. The 'life-force' of an animal or man was thought to inhere in its blood; its shedding was the escape of that life-force from its physical prison so that it became available for new spiritual ends. The blood-shedding in sacrifice was the means for the transformation of the life of the victim from one level to another.

Secondly, the *priest* did not slay the victim: this was done by the lay-worshipper: what the priest did was to take the blood (which was the life) and place it, or sprinkle it, on the altar, where by fire it was consumed so that, transformed into the element of smoke, it 'went up' to God. When it is further remembered that the victim was not offered instead of the worshipper, but was representative of the worshipper, and, as it were, carried the worshipper's own life into the presence of God, the true object of at least Jewish sacrifice becomes clearer. Sacrifice was not mere slaughter, but dedication, and the means by which human life could be brought into contact with God. Further, the fact that only an animal without physical defect (unblemished) could be employed as a victim and become the vehicle of man's self-offering stresses the notion that man felt himself too impure to enter God's presence in person, but must look for a go-between, a mediator.

But the sacrifice was not complete with the burning of the victim's blood. The offerer ate a portion of the victim and another portion was burned. In this act the offerer, as it were, sat down to table with God and enjoyed communion with Him. This last act was the climax of the sacrifice and the aim of all the preliminaries.

While such a form of worship, with all its unpleasant accompaniments, could not but be distasteful and even revolting to contemporary man, it will be seen to enshrine notions which in themselves are of imperishable value. The human consciousness of unworthiness of fellowship with God; the belief that worship must cost a man something and that only what is perfect will do (shown in the insistence upon an unblemished victim); the acknowledgement that life must be transformed before contact with God is possible, and the confession that fellowship with God is man's true end—all this the Jewish rite of sacrifice hammered into human consciousness from year to year.

Yet, when all is said, it remains true that Jewish sacrifice could not by itself *effect* anything except a realization of those truths. It was, in its objective aspect, a make-believe system, a solemn aspiration, a dramatization of hopes and longings. It could not really bring about what it symbolized. The old sacrificial system could 'never with those sacrifices which they offered year by year continually, make the comers thereunto perfect. . . . For it is not possible that the blood of bulls and of goats should take away sins.'[2] Its value lay in the work of steady preparation of God's people for what was to come; it trained the human head and heart in a ritual pattern which would one day be 'fulfilled' and given objective substance

[2] Heb. 10.1 and 4

and reality. The sacrificial lamb taken 'from the sheep or from the goats' would one day be replaced by 'the Lamb of God'.

## The Sacrifice of Christ

Unfamiliarity with the Old Testament is one reason why many people to-day fail to see how deeply the New Testament is permeated with the belief that sacrifice is man's one means of approach to God. A hurried and superficial reading of the Gospels in the light of contemporary secular moralism is another. Yet the witness, not only of the Epistle to the Hebrews, but also of the Gospels and the other Epistles, not to speak of the Apocalypse, is that our Lord thought of His mission in terms of sacrifice,[3] and that the apostolic Church accepted it as such. In Chapter II of this book an attempt was made to show that our Lord's life, death and exaltation can be viewed as the offering once for all of that perfect worship which the Father's love demands, a worship into which sinful man can be drawn and so achieve salvation. It is necessary now to show in what way that perfect worship is sacrificial worship, and how it answered to the expectations aroused by the Jewish system of sacrifice.

It must first be realized that in Christ's sacrifice He is both priest and victim. The Epistle to the Hebrews applies to our Lord the words of Psalm 40:

> 'Sacrifice and offering thou wouldest not, but a body didst thou prepare for me: In whole burnt offerings and sacrifice for sins thou hadst no pleasure: Then said I, Lo, I am come (in the roll of the book it is written of me) to do thy will, O God.'

The old sacrifices involving a human priest and an animal

[3] In his *Doctrines of the Creed*, Canon Quick sums up by saying: 'Of the types of objective theory (of the Atonement) we ... have found the most satisfactory to be that which most clearly bases itself on sacrificial ideas, and finds in the sin-offerings of the Old Testament a true foreshadowing of the Atonement'; p. 236.

victim are ineffectual: in the new sacrifice Christ is the priest offering Himself in the body God had prepared for Him. 'The Son of man came ... to give His life a ransom[4] for many.'[5] For the priest not only offers to God, but he offers on behalf of others, so that others may benefit. Again, in sacrifice to God only a perfect victim was allowable, the Lamb must be physically without blemish. Christ the priest 'in all points tempted like as we are, yet without sin'[6] offered His sinless being, a perfect humanity, to the Father, on behalf of us sinners.

Though not the end and consummation of sacrifice, death is yet a means to sacrifice, a stage in the offering which must be accomplished. The endurance of a violent death is at once the evidence of the will of the victim to give to the uttermost and also the inevitable fate awaiting a sinless being in a sinful world.[7] But the priest did not slay the victim: the priest took the blood and put it on the altar: the layman on whose behalf the priest offered did the slaying. So Christ, as priest, did not slay Himself; He was 'delivered up into the hands of men'.[8] But neither did He avoid this end, for He deliberately went to Jerusalem, knowing what awaited Him, where He both challenged and provoked it. Death did not take Him unawares, as a hapless victim of circumstances; it was not a set-back to His plans: it was a vocation, a destiny, which He seized upon; it was, in the words of Moses and Elijah at the Transfiguration, a 'decease'[9] which He 'accomplished' at Jerusalem. 'Therefore doth the Father love me, because I lay down my life, that I may take it again. No one taketh it away from me but I lay it down of myself.'[10]

The victim was not anciently slain *upon* the altar. It was

[4] The word ransom has been a puzzle to people owing to wrong ideas, e.g. a ransom paid to God, or in some early Fathers, a ransom paid to Satan. The real idea behind the word and the verb is simply ' deliverance at a great cost '—in the case of our Lord, His death and what followed it.
[5] Mark 10.45.　　[6] Heb. 4.15.　　[7] See page 22.　　[8] Luke 9.44.
[9] Both AV and RV give ' decease ', but RV margin gives ' departure '. It denotes not only death but removal from the visible order and so includes the Resurrection and Ascension (Luke 9.31).
[10] John 10.17 and 18.

slain near the altar and its blood, the sacrificed life, was taken *to* the altar after the death. So the cross on Calvary was not the altar on which Christ was sacrificed. The altar is in heaven and thither Christ was exalted after His death and Resurrection. He took His human nature, transformed, into the heavenly places and there presents His sacrifice; for 'Christ entered not into a holy place made with hands . . . but into heaven itself, now to appear before the face of God for us ',[11] where also ' he ever liveth to make intercession for them that draw near unto God through him '.[12]

In bold outline this is how the life and death and exaltation of Christ must be understood as the offering of sacrifice for man, and as the fulfilment of the ancient law of sacrifice. It will be seen how remote this great action of our Redeemer is from that caricature of sacrifice when conceived as slaughter which was in itself pleasing to God, and how in truth death is ancillary, and even incidental, to sacrifice. S. Bernard said somewhere, '*Non mors, sed voluntas sponte morientis placuit Deo*', which may be paraphrased as ' It was not death, but the voluntary obedience of him who freely gave his life which was pleasing to God '. ' To obey is better than sacrifice,' said Samuel to Saul, but the essence of our Lord's sacrifice is ' obedience unto death ', a giving to the Father on man's behalf that perfect obedience which the love of God demands, enduring the full consequences of obedience and taking that obedient human nature into heaven.

It may now be asked how man can benefit by Christ's sacrifice. Christ by His sacrifice has taken human nature into the Father's presence. But how can we get there? What keeps us out of the Father's presence is our inner condition of sinfulness. On what terms can our Father receive us, whatever Christ has done, if we are still sinners? Why should our Father take a different view of our condition because the Son has offered Himself in sacrifice for us?

This question has partly been answered in Chapter II. We are Christians because we have been baptized into Christ,

[11] Heb. 9.24.   [12] Heb. 7.25.

In that sacrament we are made members of Christ, members of His mystical body. We share in Christ's perfect humanity. We are no longer external to Him nor He to us. He is no longer only a Presence near us. He is no longer related to us as a mere historical figure. What He did in Galilee and Jerusalem in the first century A.D. is not for us just a happening in time which now may produce mental or emotional reactions. What He did there is an eternal present to us in which we share. 'All we who were baptized into Christ Jesus were baptized into his death. We were buried therefore with him through baptism into death: that like as Christ was raised from the dead through the glory of the Father so we also might walk in newness of life.'[13] In so far as Christ's Cross and Resurrection are 'past history', they are now our past history also. We are intimately one with those stages in our Lord's sacrifice. We are one with Christ also in the later stages of that sacrifice in that God has 'raised us up with him and made us to sit with him in the heavenly places, in Christ Jesus'.[14] The Father sees us only as 'in Christ'. His goodness covers all our sins. The Father knows that as long as we remain 'in Christ' we are 'being saved', we are progressively purged of our sins so long as we 'abide in' Him. And seeing this He accepts us, He justifies us, He forgives 'through' Christ, who as our Good Shepherd leads us to the everlasting fold.

In the Eucharist we continually 'plead' this one eternal sacrifice and by faith identify ourselves with it. We do not merely claim the merits of Christ's act as of something done by someone quite other than ourselves with whom we are connected only by gratitude. But as Christ eternally offers that sacrifice of perfect loving obedience begun on earth, we who are in Him, offer ourselves continually with Him, seeking by His grace to grow in that loving obedience which is the moral content of our Lord's own perpetual offering.

It will be seen from this that the Eucharist is no repetition of Christ's sacrifice, still less a repetition of His death on the

[13] Rom. 6.3 and 4.      [14] Eph. 2.6.

Cross. Even if His death could be repeated there would be no need to repeat it. It is enough that 'the Lamb' stands in heaven 'as though it had been slain'. We who because we are Christians 'have been crucified with Christ' join with Him in the Eucharist and 'proclaim the Lord's death' before the world and before the Father, but we do not need to try to repeat it. What we especially do at the Eucharist is to join in the last and everlasting stage of sacrifice, we 'eat and drink at his table in his Kingdom'.[15]

[15] See Luke 22.30.

# VIII

# THE ORDER OF THE HOLY COMMUNION

WHEN considering this Prayer Book service certain thoughts must be kept in mind. The Prayer Book was compiled under the conviction that the medieval Latin services were not only unintelligible to the laity on account of their language, but that they had been shown to be in themselves too patient of certain grave abuses and of departures from 'the decent order of the ancient Fathers' to continue in use as they were. This was especially felt about the Eucharist. In Chapter VI stress was laid upon the facts that the service had somewhat lost its earlier character of a community act, in which priest and people co-operated, and also that the Holy Sacrament was normally not received except by the celebrating priest. But an even more serious misgiving was felt about the theory of sacrifice which the medieval rite was believed to foster. Reference has already been made[1] to a fear lest a sacrificial doctrine must in the end imply that in every celebration of the Eucharist Christ is offered *afresh* and that our Lord must be thought of as in some sense repeating Calvary. That this was widely believed in the Middle Ages cannot be doubted, and the reference of Article 31, not to 'the sacrifice of the Mass', but to 'the sacrifices of Masses', is evidence of the dread of the Anglican reformers in this regard. All the more remarkable therefore is the fairly close following of the ancient structure by the new service, and the retention therein of the very word sacrifice which had become so widely and seriously misunderstood.

[1] p. 80.

## THE ORDER OF THE HOLY COMMUNION 89

In spite of their fears of the dangers thought to be inherent in the Latin order, the compilers of the Prayer Book Eucharist did not allow themselves to be stampeded into revolutionary action. They resolutely held to the old landmarks, though their horizon was not bounded by the medieval Sarum rite. Other rites of Western Christendom were drawn upon and even, in at least one instance, those of the Orthodox Eastern Church. A substantial use was made of some of the Continental Protestant orders of service, though this did not seriously touch the more important elements of the Eucharist.

The Order of the Holy Communion which is in common use to-day[2] was published in 1662. It had been preceded by the two Orders published in the reign of Edward VI (the revisions of 1559 and 1604 affected the Eucharist very little). The present Order therefore closely follows that of 1552, though some of its more notable defects are remedied.

The service falls into two sections: from the beginning till the end of the Prayer 'for Christ's Church militant here upon earth', and from the invitation 'Ye that do truly'[3] till the Blessing. This division is very ancient and the two parts were once called *Missa Catechumenorum* and *Missa Fidelium*. There was a time when those who had not the status of communicants were dismissed at the end of the first part, only the baptized and confirmed being allowed to remain for the Eucharist proper.

The Prayer Book service (first half) begins with the Lord's Prayer and the Collect 'for Purity' which together form the act of Preparation for the whole service. It is derived from the ancient form of the priest's preparation, which did not concern the laity; but this type of sectional activity the Prayer Book here and elsewhere discourages[4]: the whole service

---

[2] The Alternative Order of 1928, though a high degree of authority can rightly be claimed for its use, is not dealt with here, since, *in its entirety*, it is much less commonly used in English churches.

[3] The long Exhortation which precedes this has everywhere dropped out of use for many years.

[4] And so does the Liturgical Movement in the contemporary Roman Church.

should be the act of the whole congregation, priest and people. The Ten Commandments follow, 'farced' or inter-larded with the prayer 'Lord have mercy upon us,' etc. This provision combined a revival of the reading of an Old Testament lesson at the Eucharist before the Epistle and Gospel (it had never quite died out) with the maintenance of the long-accustomed *Kyrie Eleison*[5] (itself the relic of a long litany at this point). Modern fashion is suspicious of the Ten Commandments and they are not read as often as they profitably could be. Their place is taken by the Summary of the Law (virtually an alternative Old Testament lesson), or with *Kyrie Eleison*, recited in English or Greek.[5a]

The Collect for the Queen succeeds the Commandments and for this also there is a strange distaste to-day. It is vaguely thought to be 'Erastian' to take much notice of the Sovereign in public worship. Bishop Gore once said, 'Erastianism is a name which describes the parody of an ideal which is in itself noble, and deep-rooted in the ancient tradition of the Church and Nation'. The ideal referred to is known as 'Regalism', which regards the Queen as the first ecclesiastical person of her kingdom and the guardian and protector of the Church, positions which she occupies in virtue of her Coronation when she is consecrated to this high office. When praying for the Queen we pray at the same time for all those who exercise lawful authority in the land under the Queen's sanction, being thu powers that be, ordained of God'. The Collect for the Queen used to *follow* the Collect of the Day, but to avoid too many turnings of pages it was in 1662 placed immediately after the Commandments.

After the Collect for the Queen comes the variable Collect of the Day. In the Calendar the year is divided into a number of seasons, each with its special feasts or fasts and its series of Sundays. For each of these a special Collect, Epistle and Gospel is provided which in their own way emphasize the special commemoration desired on that particular day. Simi-

---

[5] The Greek for 'Lord have mercy'.
[5a] As allowed in the Alternative Order.

larly, though unconnected with the seasons, a series of saints' days is scattered over the year, for which a like provision is made. Nobody is certain why a collect is so called: but the word describes a brief prayer, compiled in a definite literary form, which confines itself generally to a single, but sometimes to a twofold, petition. The series of collects in the Prayer Book for the Sundays, feasts and fasts of the year are a precious collection, a legacy from very early times which, in their English translation, Bishop Sanderson of Lincoln pronounced to be 'the most passionate, proper, and most elegant comprehensive expressions that any language ever afforded'. As to their devotional content Dr. William Bright sums them up as

> 'perpetually insisting on the absolute necessity of Grace, the Fatherly tenderness of God, the might of the all-prevailing Name; which are never weak, never diluted, never drawling, never ill-arranged, never a provocation to listlessness'.

The Epistle is read after the Collects and though it is usually an extract from a veritable Epistle, it is sometimes a reading from the Acts of the Apostles, or the Apocalypse, or even from the Old Testament. At a sung service, a hymn or psalm is often interpolated here.

The Gospel follows and its reading is the climax of the first part of the service. It symbolizes Christ standing in the midst of His Church teaching still as He taught in Galilee and Jerusalem. That is why all stand and turn towards the reader and why many bless themselves with the sign of the Cross: the bishop removes his mitre, as anciently kings took off their crowns. The Nicene Creed, which is now sung or said, is the Church's 'response' to the Gospel. It is a formal recital, mainly of the events in the drama of our redemption, to which the congregation gives vocally its adherence and which constitutes an act of praise most fitting as a prelude to the Eucharistic action in the second part.

A sermon should then follow and usually does follow at

all 'solemn'[6] celebrations of the Holy Communion. Though technically the first part of the service does not end till the Offertory and the Prayer for the Church are over, yet it will be convenient to consider these in connection with the Eucharistic action with which they seem more closely connected. For the moment let us look back on the service up till the close of the sermon and see what is its purpose and how it contributes to the second part.

In a previous chapter reference was made to the importance of *edification* in public worship in the eyes of the Prayer Book's authors. This element had been fully recognized in early days and the composition of the first part of the Eucharistic office is evidence of that fact. Only when the language in which it was written became for most men unknown did the *Missa Catechumenorum* lose this character. The early part of the service for the most part makes it appeal to the understanding. The Scripture readings and the sermon provide us with material which the mind can, as it were, turn into worship, with the aid of the affections and of the will. Unless the mind is trained to keep in the foreground one or two leading aims, the fervour of worship is apt to be dissipated and efforts will end in a vague 'religiosity' which accomplishes little. The purpose of the early part of the Eucharistic Order is that by the reading of the Scriptures and the preaching of the Word these 'leading aims' may be supplied, resulting in a worship more deliberate in its intention and more unanimous in its communal aspect. Within fairly wide limits the congregation is encouraged to approach the Sacrifice with a common intention. The special context in which the Eucharistic oblation is offered on a particular day is set forth in the Scripture lessons and brought home to the people through the Sermon. It is not really enough to

---

[6] This means a celebration at which all the resources of the community are brought to bear upon the service, e.g. the use of music, a fuller ceremonial, attendance upon the priest of a number of other clergy, or lay ministers, to each of whom some special function is delegated; as opposed to celebrations, usually in the early morning, when little of such provision can normally be made.

approach the altar with an undifferentiated Christian background in the mind and imagination. What is needed is a sharp cutting edge on the mind, affections and will, and this it is the aim of the first half of the service to supply.

After the Sermon (or Nicene Creed) comes the Offertory. Though technically within the first half of the service, it is nevertheless the first stage in the sacrificial action and belongs more to what follows than to what has gone before. The Offertory is the ritual act of correspondence with our Lord's act in the Upper Room 'He took bread', 'He took the cup', and it refers to the 'placing upon the Table so much Bread and Wine' as is needed for the Communion. But in order that this action shall be shared by all the people, a collection of money is *first* made and 'reverently brought' to the priest. Out of this money the bread and wine needed are bought and the poor are relieved. This collection of money, which is indeed part of the Offertory,[7] takes the place of a much earlier custom in which the people themselves made individual offerings of bread and wine for the service and other gifts in kind for the poor. The ceremony emphasized, and, as an offering of money, still emphasizes, the inseparable connection which must exist between what the priest does and what the people do. To put your offering in the plate[8] is to take your share in putting the bread and wine on the altar. As the worshipper of old brought the sacrificial victim himself to the priest, and identified himself with it by placing his hands upon it, so the Christian by bringing his money, symbolically places his hands upon the bread and wine—not that the bread and wine are the victim, but rather the outward sign with

---

[7] Apart from the Eucharist a collection of alms is wrongly described if called 'an offertory', though the practice is all too common.

[8] The collection of money at the Offertory has a further significance. The rubric specifies that this collection shall be for the poor. Commenting on the gifts in kind for the poor in the early liturgy, L'Estrange (Alliance, ed: 1658, p. 187) says: 'These have a warrant of Attorney from God himself to receive our Alms . . . so that when we come together to break bread, in the Scripture notion, that is, to communicate, we must break it to the hungry, to God himself, in his poor members.' (Quoted by Dr. J. H. Srawley in *Liturgy and Worship*, S.P.C.K., p. 321.)

which the Divine victim will choose to associate Himself when He consecrates it by His Word. In the Offertory, therefore, the bread and wine are the symbols of our own self-offering: they represent the oblation of our own lives, our praise, our thanksgiving, our penitence, our place in the world, our property, our work, our joy and sorrow; our hopes and our love; all these we lift up to God praying that the Father will accept them as exclusively His in Christ, through whose sacrifice alone He is able to do so.

The first part of the service then closes with the recitation of the Prayer for the Church. Regarded as the close of the 'Ante-Communion', it may be considered as consigning all the activities of God's people in this world into the Divine keeping before departing. Regarded as a prelude to what follows, it is rather a gathering in of all the Church on earth to take its place round the heavenly altar. Whether the clause in which the departed are mentioned and prayer made 'that with them we may be partakers of thy heavenly Kingdom' is to be construed as prayer for the departed, the reader must decide for himself. This prayer also includes an offering to God of 'our alms and oblations' and again the reader must decide whether oblations at least includes the bread and wine just placed upon the altar, thus making public and corporate the hitherto private Offertory prayers that the celebrant or people may offer.

The first act of the priest in the second part of the service is to invite the people to 'draw near'. Doubtless these words were inserted primarily on practical grounds. It is said that the early post-Reformation Anglican custom was for the first part of the service to be read while the people were congregated in the nave or body of the church. But at this point the celebrant invites the people to take their places in the chancel so that they may be in close proximity to the Holy Table and more conveniently disposed for the reception of the Sacrament. This appears highly probable. But the significance of the words 'draw near' is not thereby exhausted. The ritual approach to the altar by the worshipper bringing his victim was a definite stage in the offering of sacrifice among the Jews, while the actual phrase 'draw near' is used several times in the Epistle to the Hebrews when alluding to our part in the sacrifice of Christ.[9] The occurrence of the words at this point, especially when coupled with the injunction to make confession of sin, is an eloquent reminder of what we are about and how we ought to do it. Though we are already identified with Christ in our baptism and crucified with Him by faith, yet our continual sins have weakened our union with Him. Each time we approach the altar we must in a way begin again at the beginning and by confession and repudiation of our sins seek to be re-identified with our Lord as we come to plead His Sacrifice. This indeed is the whole object of the Eucharist and of the successive acts of Communion we make through our lives. Though in one sense we indeed 'sit with him in the heavenly places, in Christ Jesus',[10] in another we fall continually from grace and, like the prodigal son, we again 'draw near' our Father's house seeking forgiveness and restoration through the one sacrifice of Christ.

The Invitation is followed by the Confession and Absolution. If some feel that the declaration that 'the burden of them [our sins] is intolerable' is an overstatement, let them remember that the words of the Liturgy express what we ought to feel rather than what we actually do feel when we first use them. We make them our own by aspiration, by desiring that they *may* be true of us. Further, we make our confession as members of the Church, 'members one of another' we confess not only our own private sins, but the sins which our own pride and selfishness have led others to commit, our share in that whole aggregate of sin which all but crushed our Master in the Garden of Gethsemane. Intolerable is no overstatement except to the heedless. The Absolution and Comfortable Words follow. Some think that it would be an advantage if the Prayer of Humble Access ('We do not presume,' etc.) followed the Comfortable Words, as they do in

[9] Heb. 4.16; 7.25; 10.1; 10.22.      [10] Eph. 2.6.

the 1928 service, thus bringing all the penitential part together: others prefer the alternation of praise and penitence secured by the 1662 order.

The central act of the service begins with an outburst of praise preceded by a 'fervent dialogue' between priest and people: 'Lift up your hearts,' etc., and this is a feature universal in classic Liturgies. It is an invitation to the heavenly courts, where the Sacrifice of Christ is unceasingly offered, to that radiant sanctuary where the Lamb of God, glorious yet 'as it had been slain' presents Himself to the Father amid the praises of the angels and the chorus of worship from every created thing. People sometimes speak of the Eucharist as significant in that Christ 'comes down' in our midst, upon our earthly altars. And this is true, in a sense; we must never forget that He is the Good Shepherd who still 'comes down' to seek His lost sheep and bring them home. But He comes down in order to take us up. Heaven, rather than Bethlehem, Galilee or Jerusalem, is the 'place' of His Sacrifice where we are now led to join Him, and where we sing with 'angels and archangels and all the company of heaven' the *Trisagion* of praise. Lest we should by this act of adoration be 'exalted overmuch'[11] we remember once more our sinful, creaturely, nature and use at this point the Prayer of Humble Access.

We then enter the holiest part of the service. It begins with the Prayer of Consecration. This is followed by the Communion of Priest and People: the Lord's Prayer is then said, after which the prayer beginning 'O Lord and heavenly Father' (commonly called the Prayer of Oblation) succeeds.[12] These three prayers represent for us the Canon of the Eucharist, the term being originally used to describe the fixed rule of the Eucharist which is never altered. Though the

[11] II Cor. 12.7.
[12] An alternative Prayer of Thanksgiving may be said, but though this is permitted, its use results in the abandonment of many valuable elements universal in the classic rites of Christendom. Mr. C. Leo Berry in his recent pamphlet, *A Plea for the Prayer of Oblation* (Alcuin Club), Mowbray's, discusses this dilemma most clearly.

## THE ORDER OF THE HOLY COMMUNION

Prayer Book contains almost all the features of the Canons of the classic Christian liturgies, it is unique in its inclusion within its Canon of the Communion of Priest and People, which it usually wholly precedes. Let us examine the prayers in detail.

The Consecration of the bread and wine is regarded as a necessary event for which prayer must be explicitly offered. Most of the new rites at the Reformation were content with the bare reading of the Scriptural account of the Last Supper. But in the Prayer Book a '*Prayer* of Consecration' is enjoined. This prayer begins with a thankful commemoration before God of the sacrifice offered by Christ for sinful man (in which death upon the Cross is specially emphasized), and also for our Lord's act in securing that this sacrifice shall be enshrined in 'a perpetual memory'. Some explanation of these words 'memory' and 'commemoration' is necessary.

> 'The modern notion of "remembering", psychologically viewed as the act of an individual mind, is quite alien to the Hebrew conception, which is in the first place communal. . . . When therefore Jesus said, "Do this in remembrance of me" . . . He was assuredly not planning merely to keep before his disciples' minds that which they could anyhow never forget; it was to be a "concrete remembering", a bringing back out of the past into the present—of what? Not of sins, for by His Sacrifice they are taken away. But of the Sacrifice itself, or rather of *Him*, crucified, risen from the dead, victorious through death.'[13]

The prayer then becomes explicit in the petitions which follow the words 'hear' and 'grant'; we ask that God will so act that, *when* we eat and drink, *what* we eat and drink will be the Body and Blood of Christ: and lest what we pray for should seem outrageous, the warrant for such request is fully set out by recalling what our Lord did and said in the Upper Room.

'All things whatsoever ye pray and ask for, believe that ye have received them, and ye shall have them.'[14] Having prayed that receiving these 'creatures of bread and wine' we may be 'partakers of his most blessed Body and Blood' we then eat

---

[13] A. G. Hebert in *A Theological Word Book of the Bible*, pp. 142-3 (S.C.M. Press). [14] Mark 11.24.

and drink, the priest first and the people after. 'The Body and Blood of Christ are verily and indeed taken and received by the faithful in the Lord's supper.'[15] Not simply received, in the sense that if a man's faith were strong enough, what he received might be different from, and greater than, what a man of less, or no, faith might receive. But 'taken', for it is the Body and Blood of the Lord independently of any man's reception thereof. The communicants having received the holy gifts must now 'feed on him in their hearts by faith with thanksgiving'. Their faith has not made the gift, but through faith alone they must now appropriate the *benefits* of that gift. By faith they share in all that Christ is and does, and what they have especially come to do is to share in the offering of Christ's eternal sacrifice, to join the offering of the sacrifice of themselves with the sacrifice of their Lord, now present in them and they in Him.

The Lord's Prayer is now recited, as it always is in the Prayer Book whenever any new spiritual status has been achieved, e.g. immediately after the act of baptism, after the laying on of hands at confirmation, after the joining together in holy matrimony.

Then follows the prayer called commonly the Prayer of Oblation in which, the formal consummation of sacrifice is solemnly set forth, the actual offering or oblation to God. What is it that we offer? The Prayer speaks first of 'our sacrifice of praise and thanksgiving'. It is by some imagined that the sacrifice we offer is simply a metaphorical sacrifice, a lifting up of hearts stirred to thankfulness and praise by the memory of what Christ has done for us in His death and passion.[16] Sacrifice of praise[17] and thanksgiving would mean to them a sacrifice of which the whole content was exclusively words of praise and thanksgiving, sincerely spoken. But

[15] Prayer Book Catechism.
[16] I recall the words of an American Protestant missionary who, commenting on a celebration of Holy Communion on Easter Day as strange, added: 'We always consider it a rather sad service unsuitable to a day of rejoicing.'
[17] See Heb. 13.15 where 'sacrifice of praise' is a translation of the Hebrew denoting the highest form of the peace offering.

'It is impossible to regard the phrase "of praise and thanksgiving" as other than adjectival. Just as "Father of heaven" (*Pater de coelis, Pater coelestis*) means heavenly Father, so "sacrifice of praise and thanksgiving" means "laudable and eucharistic sacrifice". Tradition apart, in the Anglican rite in England (except the 1927-28 Alternative) praise is rare and thanksgiving almost entirely absent. It is therefore impossible to accept the belief that the sacrifice here offered is an offering of certain praises and thanksgiving, which offering is quite distinct from the Eucharistic Sacrifice.'[18]

What we offer therefore is an offering which, in itself and independently of the words which accompany it, constitutes the supreme act of praise and thanksgiving. The nature of this offering is unfolded later in the prayer when we say: 'And here we offer and present unto Thee, O Lord, ourselves, our souls and bodies, to be a reasonable, holy, and lively, sacrifice unto Thee.'

The offering then is just the offering of our own imperfect humanity to God? No. Not *just* ourselves. For we who offer ourselves have 'verily and indeed taken and received' the Body and Blood of Christ. We have thereby been taken up into Him and we offer ourselves to the Father in Christ's eternal offering of Himself. 'Where is the Sacrifice in the English Communion Service?' asked Professor Burkitt.

'Surely in this, that the congregation having confessed, been shriven, having "assisted" at a due consecration of the bread and wine, and finally having received their own portion, do then and there offer unto God themselves, their souls and bodies, to be a reasonable sacrifice. *By what has gone before* [italics mine] so far as ritual both of words and actions can effect anything at all, the congregation have been hallowed into the Body of Christ.'[19]

The prayer calls this sacrifice 'our bounden duty and service'.

[18] C. Leo Berry, *op. cit.*, pp. 14 and 15.
[19] *Eucharist and Sacrifice*, by E. Crawford Burkitt. Heffer, 1921.

Surely this is right, for by this sacramental identification of ourselves with Christ's perfect sacrifice and the offering of the whole to God we accomplish our human destiny, we are brought into the presence of God Himself where we truly belong but from which our sins had excluded us. God accepts us in Christ and because of Christ, and so the Prayer ends with the great doxology 'through Jesus Christ our Lord by whom and with whom, in the unity of the Holy Ghost, all honour and glory be unto thee, O Father Almighty, world without end. Amen'.

It will be seen therefore that through devout and faithful participation in the Holy Communion the end achieved is the end to which the ancient sacrifices looked longingly, but to which they were powerless really to lead their worshippers. This end is communion with God, fellowship with the All-Holy one, made possible in the Eucharist because our Victim really does take away the sins of the world.

Nor must another result of this Christian sacrifice be forgotten. It was explained above that the essence of the Eucharistic Sacrifice is the offering of itself by the whole Church, the Head and its members to God. Each individual worshipper is 'hallowed into the Body of Christ' so that each is one, not only with the Head, but with all the other members of the Body. It is communion of man with man as well as of man with God. This fact is witnessed in remarkable words in the Prayer of Thanksgiving (which follows the Prayer of Oblation as an alternative[20]) which speaks of those who have communicated as 'very members incorporate in the mystical body of thy Son, which is the blessed company of all faithful people'. Remembrance of this more constantly in private preparation for Holy Communion, so that this unity is not only achieved sacramentally but realized progres-

---

[20] Professor Burkitt, *op. cit.*, p. 23, says: 'The only change I would make in the present Communion Service is to change the Rubric "*or this*" (between the Prayer of Oblation and the Prayer of Thanksgiving) into "*and this*" ending the second prayer . . . without repeating the doxology.'

sively in its achievement, would do much for the spiritual health of God's Church.

The service ends with the hymn known as *Gloria in excelsis*. No other rite has ever placed this hymn in that position and in the Latin rites, both modern and medieval, it is used between *Kyrie Eleison* and the Collects. In the Prayer Book it becomes a Thanksgiving, all the more necessary where the Prayer of Oblation is used after the Our Father. It is sometimes urged that we should follow the wider tradition of Western Christendom and use it at the beginning on the grounds that the opening words 'Glory be to God on high,' etc., occur in the song sung by angels at our Lord's birth. Therefore, as representing Christmas, the hymn should come previous to the parts of the service which represent Good Friday and Easter. Yet, though the hymn begins with a reference to the angels' song at Christmas, it commemorates the Lamb of God who takes away sin and ends with His exaltation 'most high in the glory of God the Father'. And the majority of Anglicans would hardly like to part with what has become their act of Thanksgiving for Holy Communion, which has, after centuries of use in our Church in this position, fully justified the change which Cranmer made. With what better act of worship could a Christian end the sacrifice than with the words 'For thou only art holy, thou only art the Lord, thou only, O Christ, with the Holy Ghost, art most high in the glory of God the Father.[21] Amen'.

The Service now being ended, a blessing is here provided as an intimation that all are free to depart.

[21] The late Dr. Geoffrey Shaw, sometime chief inspector of music at the Board of Education, wrote in an unpublished paper: 'There must be a kind of frenzy of adoration in worship. Think for a moment of the intensity and glow of the last section of *Gloria in excelsis*: "For thou only art holy," etc. Note the accumulative force of the use of the word "only" three times. Note the numerical preponderance of strong vowel sounds. Above all, note the running, lilting rhythm. It is impossible to recite this section without a springing heart, and a lively sense of worship.'

# IX

# MORNING AND EVENING PRAYER

THESE two services, also called Mattins[1] and Evensong, belong to a class of liturgical prayer called 'offices' and, in full, 'choir-offices'. They are non-sacramental services consisting of psalms, Bible-lessons and prayers. Office comes from the Latin word for duty. They are called choir-offices because in the greater part of Christendom to-day they are used as public services in choir mainly by communities attached to cathedrals, convents and other collegiate churches, and not by ordinary congregations in parish churches. Even in the Middle Ages, when to some extent the laity still attended some of these 'offices', they had for practical purposes become the characteristic public prayer of specialists.

And yet when the Prayer Book appeared with its daily office, consisting of two services, for the use of ordinary congregations, it was not putting forward a novelty. The origin and development of the 'Divine Office' is still obscure, yet it is known that in early times in different parts of Christendom there were two daily services[2] of this type intended for, and attended by, the laity. Yet to-day the Anglican Communion of Churches is the only section of Christendom which deliberately and systematically (and after centuries of experience) still puts this type of worship before ordinary congregations. It has become the envy of other Christians, both in the Roman

---

[1] The Prayer Book spelling of this word is here adopted, as used in the headings for the Lessons Proper to Holy Days and Sundays.
[2] See 'The Choir Offices', by E. C. Ratcliff, in *Liturgy and Worship* (S.P.C.K.).

Catholic and in the Free Churches; among the latter considerable use appears to be made of the material from Prayer Book Mattins or Evensong.

Nevertheless, in spite of the success of these services restored to us at the Reformation, very little is done to keep them cherished by and commended to the rank and file of Anglican congregations. Archbishop Davidson used to lament, so it is said, that while so much exposition and teaching was devoted to the Eucharist, so little attention was given to helping people understand Mattins and Evensong. He was right, as we, who are beginning to reap the fruit of this non-attention, can see only too well. It seems to be assumed that anyone can rationally and with profit take part in these services without any training or explanation at all. How often is the structure of these services the theme of any sermon or instruction in church? How often are congregations shown how to use the psalms, or canticles, as Christian praise? These matters are often mentioned as problems and difficulties, but instruction upon them remains infrequent. Is it because of this that decay has set in and that people acquiesce in 'shortened' Evensong (emasculated Evensong would be a more suitable name), in the reduction of Psalmody to eight or ten verses at the most, and in the multiplication of hymns of diluted theology and perilous poetry? It must be understood that if the offices of Mattins and Evensong are to continue in an age when the idiom and ethos of Holy Scripture are becoming largely unknown, it can only be done if the clergy are prepared to devote a good deal of time and effort to instruction upon them.

Something has already been said about these services in earlier chapters, particularly that each 'office' is a memorial of our Redemption and yet that, though in this way each office is complete in itself, in another way all the offices are mutually dependent upon and supplementary to one another; the unit of worship in this sense is not a single office, but a year's series of offices. This fact may be referred to again.

Though the offices are non-sacramental, they are nevertheless sacrificial, for no praise can be acceptable to God except 'through (the sacrifice of) Jesus Christ our Lord' of which fact constant affirmation is made throughout the services. The sacrifice is not sacramentally shown forth as in the Eucharist, yet a mystical participation therein is assumed throughout.

Each of the two offices begins with an identical penitential preparation, not said secretly and individually, as in the Latin rite, but recited 'with a loud voice' as a public act. It must be confessed that this preparation is somewhat cumbersome in its forms, yet it is at any rate straightforward and easy to follow in the book. The alternatives provided in the 1928 Prayer Book may be excellent in themselves, but they introduce at the start in their very variety an element of uncertainty and confusion which breaks people's confidence in the book, and causes them to discontinue trying to follow the service there. This too often leads to inattention and listlessness. It is better to have an attentive congregation using the old form ('Dearly beloved brethren' and all) than to provide forms which, however suitable, are difficult to find quickly. Liturgical worship is hard work, requiring attentiveness: anything which baffles the attempt to follow the service closely should be avoided.

It is sometimes asked whether it is a good plan to start with penitence and whether it would not be better to lead up to it at a later point in the service. There may be much to be said for the latter suggestion, but if each office is to be considered as a memorial of redemption, it is best to start from where we actually are in spiritual standing. It is just because we are sinners that we need redeeming and it would perhaps obscure that fact if we were not asked to remember it whenever we begin to worship. As the Eucharist has its *Lord have mercy upon us* at the beginning so the offices have the General Confession. The language of this confession is sometimes criticized as being more extreme than the feelings of the average worshipper can in sincerity justify, but the reader will remember what was said about a similar criticism of the Confession in the Communion service on page 95.

After the Penitential Introduction, the office both at Mattins

MORNING AND EVENING PRAYER 105

and Evensong begins at once with Psalmody, for the *Preces* (as the introductory versicles and responses are properly called) are themselves detached verses of psalms. It was in early days customary for 'offices' to begin straight away, without preamble, with the recitation of complete psalms; indeed, this is still the case in the funeral office of the Prayer Book *Order for the Burial of the Dead*. But in the daily offices selected verses of Psalms 51 and 70, together with a *Gloria*, are shared by priest and people as a sort of 'lead in' to the Psalms proper.

At Mattins Psalm 95, *Venite, exultemus Domino,* is used invariably before the Psalms of the day. This is a very ancient practice and it is called the Invitatory Psalm for obvious reasons. It comes most appropriately in this position at the beginning of a day's worship for it reminds us that the God whom we worship in the sanctuary is the God of Nature, as well as of Grace, for 'In his hand are all the corners of the earth . . . the sea is his . . . and his hands prepared the dry land'. And it further warns us that since the God of Nature is also the God of Righteousness and Truth near whom no evil can exist, we must, while hearing His voice, take pains not to 'harden our hearts' lest we find ourselves shut out of His presence. Modern sentiment, always eager to tone down or stifle the very thought of any threat to our security, has decreed that the verses of the psalm which speak of this dread possibility may be omitted, thus reversing a practice almost 1,500 years old.[3]

After *Venite* at Mattins and after the *Preces* at Evensong follows the portion of the Psalter appointed for the day. The length of the period in which the whole Psalter is gone through varies throughout Christendom. In some parts it is still, on

[3] See *The Doctrine of the Atonement*, Leonard Hodgson (Nisbet), p. 60: 'The belief that God has sworn in his wrath that men who do certain things shall not enter into his rest enables the Church to open its worship each day with the words, "Come let us sing unto the Lord, let us heartily rejoice in the strength of our salvation". It is a pity that in the American edition of the Book of Common Prayer the morning hymn of our Church has been abbreviated so as to obscure this truth, and that this bad example was followed by the English revisers in 1928.'

occasions, recited daily in its entirety; in others twice a week and in the Roman Church once a week. In the diocese of Milan it is only recited twice a month and in the Anglican Church once[4] a month. The Book of Common Prayer provides that the psalms be used in their numerical order, in daily portions, straight through. But it was from the first agreed that there should be exceptions to this and provision was made for specially selected psalms on the great feasts and fasts of the year. This principle has been carried further in recent years, so that every Sunday and many feast days now have special psalms.

Every psalm must be concluded with *Glory be to the Father, etc.*, as an affirmation 'that the same God is worshipped by Christians as by Jews; the same God that is glorified in the psalms, having been from the beginning Father, Son and Holy Ghost, as well as now'.[5]

## How to Use the Psalms

Like many other features of Church ritual and ceremonial the psalms originally seem to have taken their place in a casual and almost accidental manner, and not as the fruit of deliberate policy. Professor Burkitt says:

'We hear of psalms in public worship as soon almost as we get any definite information about Christian worship at all . . . As far as I can make out, however, the practical use to which the psalms were originally put by authority in Christian congregations was the excellent, if humble, office of filling up time, the office of occupying persons profitably who otherwise would be left idle. This really is the key to more liturgical questions than might at first sight appear. In other words, the congregations were not assembled in order to sing psalms or hymns, but, the congregations being assembled for some other

---

[4] I have only heard of one other scheme for monthly recitation, namely in the Breviary of a long extinct religious order known as the *Humiliati*. This Breviary appeared in 1548, only a few months before the first edition of the English Prayer Book.

[5] See *A Rational Illustration of the Book of Common Prayer*, Charles Wheatley.

purpose, were set to occupy themselves in singing something suitable.'[6]

Thus psalms were ordered to be sung in large congregations during the Communion of the people, and S. Athanasius, while he and his people were besieged in the church of St. Thomas at Alexandria, occupied them with selections from the Psalter. But gradually the singing of psalms became an authentic part of formal worship, and their use was regulated and imposed by authority. As such they appear in the Book of Common Prayer, no longer an interlude in the business of worship, but the very material and vehicle of worship itself.

But in what way are they to be regarded and used? It is plain that at least many of them were composed for use at Jewish ecclesiastical functions and *in their original sense* these do not apply to the situation of Christian worship. Others were written for use at, or to commemorate, what we should call a political crisis, and again, *as such*, they can hardly concern us. Others reveal misunderstandings, defects of faith, and a temper of mind inconsistent, *in their originally intended meaning*, with Christian aspiration and belief. Only a few are, as they now stand, and as originally intended, wholly suitable for true worship at all times and in all places. Yet from early days the whole Psalter has been continually and delightedly used by the Christian Church in its worship, despite the total changes of external circumstances and the great differences between Jewish and Christian faith and sentiment. How are we to continue that use?

Probably the most common way is to regard the psalms used at any service as a field in which as it were some choice flowers can be found and gathered. The searcher for flowers enters the field and, ignoring the grass and the less interesting weeds, keeps a look-out for such plants as have colour and fragrance. These he gathers and delights in their appearance and scent, lingering a little over them as he goes. Thus many

---

[6] *Christian Hymns*, F. C. Burkitt. Printed in the Proceedings of the Society of Historical Theology. Oxford, 1908.

a worshipper will approach, say, Psalm 61. He will perhaps regard the first two verses and even the third as 'grass', paying no particular attention to them. But verse 4 may appear different: 'I will dwell in thy tabernacle for ever: and my trust shall be under the covering of thy wings.' The words find a response within and perhaps, while the choir goes on with verses 5 and 6, he will in his own manner ponder over verse 4. Or the Psalm is number 93, but the words will pass over and by him until he comes to verse 5: 'The waves of the sea are mighty, and rage horribly; but yet the Lord who dwelleth on high is mightier.' The words will evoke within him a faith in the power of God which he may at once apply to some circumstance in his own life.

Nobody could deny that such an employment of the psalms is profitable; the acts of gratitude, wonder, penitence, trust which are inculcated by isolated verses are true worship and must indeed be pleasing to God. But are we to be content with this and reconciled to treating perhaps the remaining eighty-five per cent of the Psalter as mere unintelligible background to the favoured verses? What about such ejaculations which we cannot sincerely use as coming from ourselves?

> 'I will take no wicked thing in hand; I hate the sins of unfaithfulness: there shall no such cleave unto me.
> A froward heart shall depart from me: I will not know a wicked person.'[7]

Or what about the historical element in the Psalter?

> 'Our fathers regarded not thy wonders in Egypt, neither kept they thy great goodness in remembrance: but were disobedient at the sea, even at the Red Sea.
> Nevertheless, he helped them for his Name's sake: that he might make his power to be known.'[8]

How can this be profitably used as worship by a Christian to-day?

[7] Ps. 101. 4-5.   [8] Ps. 106.7-8.

Or consider again:

> 'Many oxen are come about me: fat bulls of Basan close me in on every side.
> They gape upon me with their mouths: as it were a ramping and a roaring lion.
> I am poured out like water, and all my bones are out of joint: my heart also in the midst of my body is even like melting wax.'[9]

Are such verses just to be formally chanted, with no idea of worshippers really entering into them? Must we just put up with them till we come to a passage which we can easily make our own?

The fact is that this treating of the psalms as a field in which each individual must gather his own 'nosegay of devotion' is not enough to sustain a lasting habit of using and valuing them, nor is it of great use as a method of congregational worship. 'Much harm has been done,' writes M. R. Newbolt,[10]

> 'by the habit of reciting the psalms in the same frame of mind as hymns. A hymn is a popular devotion intended to kindle a personal emotion or express an individual's sentiment; it expresses *me*, and is meant to put into words what I feel or ought as an individual to feel; as a popular devotion based on individualism it is an invaluable aid to devotion. But we cannot sing the psalms as if they were hymns.'

Then how are we to sing them?

Plainly we must learn to find more in them than meets the eye and cultivate what is sometimes called a 'mystical use' of the psalms: we must find some clue to their interpretation, some key which will unlock all the doors, revealing an inner meaning. People sometimes are apt to be suspicious when this is said and even contemptuous. When the question of the 'cursing' psalms was being discussed in the Church

---
[9] Ps. 22.12-14.
[10] *The Bible and the Ministry*, M. R. Newbolt, p. 62 (Dacre Press, 1942).

Assembly during Prayer Book Revision one speaker affected to treat with scorn and ridicule this method as applied to Ps. 137.9 and spoke with irony of 'throwing mystical children against metaphorical stones'.[11] Yet some such mystical interpretation is in fact necessary, not merely in 'cursing' psalms but throughout the Psalter. Indeed it is just as necessary in the blessings pronounced in the Psalter upon the godly. Who could contemplate without embarrassment the bursting granaries and the prolific cattle promised as a reward for godliness in Ps. 144, or the 'quiver full' of children guaranteed in Ps. 127 and 128 as the inevitable result of fearing the Lord? Unless the words are used symbolically we cannot speak of God as 'putting on glorious apparel' or as 'riding upon the Cherubim'. Therefore some inner meaning[12] must be sought by which the imagery of the psalms is translated into spiritual conceptions and some clue must be found by which they become, not merely the meditations of the individual, but the praise of the Church.

An inkling of the right method is supplied in some of the page-headings in the Authorized Version of the Psalms of David. There Ps. 45 is described as concerned with 'the Majesty and grace of Christ's Kingdom', Ps. 47 with 'the Church's confidence in God', and Ps. 110 as 'Christ's Kingdom predicted', and so on. This is the practical application of what the seventh of the Thirty-nine Articles says: 'for both in the Old and New Testament everlasting life is offered to mankind by Christ.' If the people of the Old Covenant were nourished from the psalms, as with water out of a rock,

[11] On this passage S. Augustine writes: 'Who are the little ones of Babylon? Evil desires at their birth . . . When desire is born, before evil habit has gained strength against thee. while it is still small . . . dash it. But be on your guard, lest, when it is dashed, it die not. Dash it against the rock. And the rock was Christ.'

[12] 'Now words have but one meaning, though they may have not only a two-fold but a manifold application. . . . The dispensation under which they [the Psalms] were written did not stand alone, it was part of an organism . . . not yet completed. . . . In a growing plant the relation of the parts to the whole is best discerned in the maturity, not in the infancy of the growth.' W. T. Davison in article in Hastings *Dictionary of the Bible* on Psalms, Book of (Vol. IV., p. 160, column 2).

'that rock was Christ'.[13] And did not our Lord declare that what was written in the psalms, as well as in the law and the prophets, concerned Himself?[14] Reflection upon these truths leads us then to the clue which interprets the Psalter. 'It suits every man,' said Father R. M. Benson,[15]

> 'because it is the utterance of true manhood. It expresses the true desires of a true manhood. . . . We must recognize them as being the utterance of the Incarnate Son of God, the only True Man.'

How plainly the Gospels show the truth of these words. The words of the Psalter are evidently in the forefront of Christ's mind and are frequently upon His lips: He chooses its words as the most suitable vehicle for expressing His thoughts and prayers: in the extremest moment of direction He ever knew, He pours out His agony in the words of Psalm 22: in the final moment of triumph He breathes out His joyful trust to the Father in Psalm 31.

Now 'Jesus Christ is the same yesterday, to-day, and for ever'.[16] Though exalted to the right hand of the Father in His eternal Sonship, He is still Man, not untouched 'with the feeling of our infirmities'.[17] The words of praise and trust He used in the days of His flesh are still a means by which we men can enter into His mind and heart. 'Where two or three are gathered together in my name, there am I in the midst of them.'[18] And we may surely say: Where two or three are gathered together in My name *praying*, there am I *praying* in the midst of them. And since we want to pray in Him and with Him, what better bridge can there be between Him and us than the words of the Psalter? Through them we can be sure of entering into His prayer.

This then is the clue to the way we should at least for the most part employ the Psalter. They are not my prayer, con-

---

[13] I Cor. 10.4.   [14] Luke 24.44.
[15] *War Songs of the Prince of Peace*, Vol. 1, pp. 5 and 8 (John Murray, 1901.)
[16] Heb. 13.8.   [17] Heb. 4.15.   [18] Matt. 18-20.

fined to the expression of my feelings and aspirations. They are His[19] prayer into which I may progressively enter. They do not come down to my level, they take me up to His, to the level of perfect Man, true man. When the psalm you are using says 'I' or 'me' or 'mine' it does not refer to you, as you are now, but to Him as He is and always has been. But you may join Him, and the more you join Him in spirit and in truth the more the words will be true of you also. And the Christ whom you join in the psalms is no solitary Being: He is the Lord of hosts, the Head of the Body, the Captain of the redeemed. So that the 'I' and 'me' of the psalms can also be thought of as the Church, as one in Him. The psalms are the praise of Christ in His Church, or of the Church in Christ. They are not an individual's prayer, but the prayer of the whole Body, they are the very stuff of what we prosaically call 'corporate worship'.

Apply these principles to a particular psalm, say Ps. 3. It seems easiest to regard it as the utterance of our Lord as His Passion draws near and as He begins to experience the triumph of His Resurrection.

> 'Lord, how are they increased that trouble me: . . .
> Many one there be that say of my soul: There is no help for him in his God.
> But thou, O Lord, art my defender: . . .'

And so on.

We see our Lord as the purposes of Satan (working through His earthly opponents) mature, and as His arrest draws near. He knows that His enemies will mistake His readiness to suffer for mere defenceless weakness and a proof that He is not 'of God'. We join our Lord as He holds this converse with His Father, for our own little experiences of the power of temptation and of evil, and a sense of our own weakness, enable us to enter into our Lord's mind.

---

[19] Some may consider this statement too sweeping, though the author finds year by year that used with this belief the psalms grow in depth and scope. At least the words can be received as a clue to the use of the psalms, as a statement generally true.

'I did call upon the Lord with my voice: and he heard me out of his holy hill.

I laid me down and slept, and rose up again: for the Lord sustained me.'

In Gethsemane Christ 'offered up prayers and supplications with strong crying and tears unto him that was able to save him from death, and was heard'. But he was not saved from physical dying; it was from extinction by His enemy from which He was delivered. He did indeed die: 'I laid me down and slept.' But God raised Him from the dead. Reverently and with humility we try here to enter into our Lord's mind, for He has said, 'Watch with me'. We can then try to share the joy of His victory:

... thou hast broken the teeth of the ungodly.
Salvation belongeth unto the Lord: and thy blessing is upon thy people.'

To recite this psalm is to be drawn by our Lord into the mystery of His Passion and Exaltation by which He has redeemed us and in which He offers perfect praise to His Father.

Take another example: Ps. 80. Here 'I' and 'me' are not mentioned: it is all in the plural. Christ speaks in His Church. It is a prayer of Christ in His Church to the Father ('the Shepherd of Israel') out of a condition of persecution and misery:

'Thou hast brought a vine out of Egypt: ...
Thou madest room for it: and when it had taken root it filled the land. ...
She stretched out her branches unto the sea: ...
Why hast thou then broken down her hedge? ...
The wild boar out of the wood doth root it up: and the wild beasts of the field devour it.'

The vine is, of course, the people of God, the Church; Egypt is the bondage of sin from which by God's power it has been delivered, and then greatly blessed and increased. Why is hurt and persecution allowed against what God has planted? It is the age-long cry of faith when confronted with the apparent weakness of God and the power of evil.

> 'Turn thee again, thou God of hosts, look down from heaven: behold and visit this vine; . . .
> And so will not we go back from thee: O let us live, and we shall call upon thy Name.
> Turn us again, O Lord God of hosts: show the light of thy countenance, and we shall be whole.'
>
> vv. 14, 18-19.

The vine, as said above, is the people of God, but there was a moment when our Lord was in Himself alone the people of God, the faithful remnant. So this psalm too takes us with Christ into His passion in the midst of which it seemed to Him that He did not see 'the light of the Father's countenance'. And we take into Christ's passion, all the sufferings of His Church, its endurances of persecutions, its betrayals by false brethren, its failures and weakness. We do not ask much for freedom from actual suffering, but for deliverance from that final suffering of not seeing God's face, and for strength to be loyal in all our trials.

When it is remembered that the psalms are the prayers of Christ into which we are drawn, many passages which seem insincere when regarded as my individual worship, can be used without embarrassment and indeed with a new confidence and hope, e.g.

> Whom have I in heaven but thee: and there is none upon earth that I desire in comparison of thee.
>
> Ps. 73.24.
>
> My soul is athirst for God, yea, even for the living God: when shall I come to appear before the presence of God?
> My tears have been my meat day and night: while they daily say unto me, Where is now thy God?
>
> Ps. 42.2-3.
>
> My soul shall be satisfied, even as it were with marrow and fatness: when my mouth praiseth thee with joyful lips.
>
> Ps. 63.6.

Likewise the passages which betray consciousness of being the object of antipathy and persecution, which represent the colloquy of our Lord with His Father as His antagonists begin to close upon him:

> O God, the proud are risen against me: and the congregation of naughty men have sought after my soul. . . .
> Ps. 86.14.

It may be asked how the passages which seem to betray human infirmity and frailty can be the words of the Son of God, or words which seem to express doubt of His Father's promises:

> Shall thy loving-kindness be showed in the grave? . . .
> Shall thy wondrous works be known in the dark: and thy righteousness in the land where all things are forgotten?
> Ps. 88.11-12.

But our Lord is touched with the feeling of our infirmity and though He never gave way to doubt, He could experience the power of temptation to doubt.

Mention was made above about the historical psalms, and these also have a 'relevance' for us when we think of them as our Lord's recital of God's mighty acts in the past, acts in the long process of deliverance of His people which is to culminate in His own passion and resurrection. With Him we survey the past, not as a mere chronicle of events, a valley of dry bones, but as an affirmation of faith in God's purposes and of our belief that we too are actors in this living drama of Divine Providence, not yet fully over.

It may be asked how the imprecatory, or cursing psalms, fit into this scheme. Is not their spirit wholly contrary to the tenderness and compassion of Christ? Is not the difficulty the same whether we regard them as our utterance or as His? It is hardly profitable in such a controversial matter to seek to pronounce a final opinion, but certain considerations are here put forward to assist the reader to come to his own conclusions.

These particular psalms, though they trouble modern consciences, do not seem to have disturbed any past generation of Christians.[20] A valuable book called *Songs of Zion*, by Lionel James (John Murray, 1936) provides notes on the historical use and appreciation of the psalms showing how great men in the past have valued this or that psalm. When he comes to Psalm 109 the author makes his own comment, but is apparently unable to summon any witnesses from the past to support his own disapproval of it. Does our modern shrinking from such psalms mean that we are morally and spiritually superior in this respect to all past generations of Christians? Has a new revelation been granted to us, which was withheld from them? Is our dislike due to a genuine refinement of thought and feeling, or is it just that our nerves are not so tough as our forefathers'? Or is it that we are less sensitive to sin and therefore more baffled by the notion of punishment and retribution? When we try to consider what evil is and what it deserves, we need to bear in mind this fact. We only know evil when it is mixed with good. In the worst human being we have ever met, the evil was not unalloyed. Good also was present. Would our view about the nature and deserts of evil change if we could experience evil in its nakedness, wholly unmixed with any good? That is surely how our Lord saw it in the Garden of Gethsemane. All these factors should be weighed. And the late Dr. Goudge has some useful advice:[21] 'There are words in the imprecatory psalms which as Christians we cannot take upon our lips in their original sense. But it is as easy to fall below their spirit as to rise above it; and we do fall below it when we ignore "the persecution of the poor helpless man" unless we suffer ourselves.'[22]

If therefore we use the imprecatory psalms we must think

---

[20] It is interesting to note that the first recorded use of the psalms by the Church after our Lord's Ascension was that of Ps. 69.25 (part of a 'cursing' section) and that its use by S. Peter was prefaced by the solemn words: The Holy Ghost by the mouth of David spake. See Acts 1.16-20.
[21] *The Apocalypse and the Present Age*, p. 70 (Mowbray, 1935).
[22] The reference is to Ps. 109.15.

of 'mine enemies', on whom retribution is invoked, not as the people of whom I personally disapprove, but as those to whom our Lord refers as having 'both seen and hated both me and my Father',[23] those 'that call evil good, and good evil',[24] those who, having blasphemed against the Holy Spirit, are 'guilty of an eternal sin'.[25] But perhaps the best plan is to interpret 'enemies' not as people of any sort, but as 'evil thoughts which assault and hurt the soul' or as 'spiritual wickedness in high places'. All this may present great difficulties to us and we must remember in our perplexity what Berdyaev says: 'Evil, being absolutely irrational, is therefore incapable of being grasped by reason and remains inexplicable.' As to retribution upon evil, it has been revealed to us, not that vengeance is wrong, but that 'vengeance is mine . . . saith the Lord'.[26] It is for that retribution that we are invited to pray in the psalms.

To return to the general question of how the psalms are to be used. It is hoped that enough has been said to give the main clue to their use. But it must be added that even with these thoughts in mind the psalms will continue to present difficulties. No instruction can be clear enough or sufficient enough to remove all obstacles at a stroke. The Psalms do not yield up all their secrets at the first attempt to find them. As with the rest of Holy Scripture, a lifetime of humble, patient and hopeful use is necessary for the discovery of its riches, and even then the process is incomplete. One could hardly expect it to be otherwise. The psalms are not only provided to be the vehicle of our worship but are given to us precisely in order that by the very difficulty involved in their use our powers of worship may be exercised and may grow in scope and depth.

But it must be repeated that if they are to continue to be the main substance of Anglican worship (outside the Sacraments) it can only be if frequent and thoughtful instruction is given upon their meaning and use. This should be no grievous task. What better instruction can be given than the

[23] John 15.24.  [24] Isa. 5.20.  [25] Mark 3.29.  [26] Rom. 12.19.

progressive initiation of people into this great treasury of devotion and praise? Is it possible to provide a greater help to congregations than to train them to use the psalms with the mind, emotions, and will? Clergy sometimes excuse themselves for reducing the amount of Psalmody to just a few verses by saying that the people do not understand them. They are never likely to if they are not taught, and there are few things more profitable to teach.

Some words should be said about the translation of the Psalter in the Prayer Book. It is not from the Authorized Version of 1611, but from the Great Bible of 1539. It is full of inaccuracies and mistranslations, and here and there of passages which mean little or nothing. Nevertheless, from the first it captured the affections of Englishmen. When the 'Bishops' Bible' of 1568 appeared its revised version of the Psalms met with widespread disapproval, so much so that in the second edition of the Bishops' Bible, in 1572, the Psalter was printed in parallel columns with the 1539 (Prayer Book) translation on one side and the revised one on the other. In the later editions[27] the 1539 version alone appears. Although references were from time to time made as to the inaccuracies of the Great Bible (1539) version, its prestige was so high that no suggestion was made to replace it in the Prayer Book when the Authorized Version appeared in 1611. In 1913 Archbishop Davidson appointed a committee of very learned divines to produce a conservative revision of the Prayer Book Psalter, devoting their attention to such 'passages in the Psalter in which the language is specially obscure or misleading'. This they did, but, though it was hoped to incorporate it in the Revised Prayer Book, the newly formed House of Laity threw it out in 1923.[28] The Great Bible version seems difficult to eradicate, and indeed small wonder at that for, in spite of its obvious deficiencies, it has superlative merits, not least among them being its suitability for singing. But if it is ever

[27] Except that of 1585.
[28] The Church of Ireland has taken this Revision of the Psalter into its Prayer Book and seems well satisfied with it.

to be replaced, the version of Archbishop Davidson's Committee would be the ideal substitute.

*Bible Lessons, Canticles, Suffrages and Prayers*

Both at Mattins and Evensong the psalms are followed by the reading of a lesson from the Old Testament. After the ensuing canticle or hymn comes a lesson from the New Testament.

In the Middle Ages, except at the Night Office, Bible lessons became very brief, often indeed being reduced to a single sentence. But the Prayer Book restored the use of substantial portions of Holy Scripture at these two Day Offices. What is the purpose of these public Bible readings?

They are often regarded as being solely a means by which the Church is informed and instructed in the Word of God, as messages, so to speak, from God to His people. This indeed they are and as such must be heard attentively in a receptive frame of mind. The Invitatory Psalm at Mattins prepares the way for such a use when it warns us, 'To-day if ye will hear his voice, harden not your hearts'. Bishop Winnington-Ingram (of London) was fond of saying that in the Daily Office we listen to 'four letters from heaven'. We would miss an essential part of a Christian's worship if we ever overlooked this 'waiting upon God's Word' in the Lessons. But all the same the use of Scripture has a complementary purpose in public worship. For worship is an activity of love and true love always consists of the twofold movement of both receiving and giving. There should always be a 'two-way traffic' in all acts of worship.

Thus while we attentively listen for God's voice, at the same time we give praise for what we hear. The Lessons are therefore occasions for a real hearkening, in a receptive and meditative spirit, and also for a giving back to God, in the proclamation of His mighty works, of the honour due to Him. It is not possible to lay down any hard and fast rule, but while some books are read, e.g. the Epistles, the predominant function of the congregation will be hearing, but in the case of other books, e.g. the historical books, it will be as an act of praise that they will chiefly be read. And whatever is being read the need for very close attention is essential. It used to be far more common than it now is for the congregation to follow the lessons in their Bibles. In these days of radio, when our ears are so constantly assailed with words, and in which we unconsciously develop a habit of hearing without listening, we need all the more to take steps really to listen, when it is imperative that we should. Too often the reading of the lessons becomes a mere interlude of relaxation between the periods of singing, and the Bible is read to an assembly which, if it does not harden its heart, at least suffers its ears to be stopped.

It would be at any rate a step in the direction of encouraging people to follow the lessons in Bibles if the lessons were announced in a more helpful way. The 1662 book directs that the verse shall be announced first, then the chapter, then the book, a method which all but paralyses the memory of the listener who wants to find the place. The 1928 rubric reverses the order, putting the book first, then the chapter, then the verse, thus assisting the mental process involved in finding the place. It would be valuable if this method were more generally adopted.

The first lesson over, we pass, in our Memorial of Redemption, from the Old Covenant to the New. At Mattins *Te Deum Laudamus* (called a hymn) is sung[29] and at Evensong the Song of the Blessed Virgin Mary called *Magnificat*. Each is intended to be an act of praise for the fulfilment in the Christian dispensation, of God's promises to the people of old, thus leading on to the Second Lesson from the New Testament. This in turn is succeeded by another canticle, *Benedictus* at Mattins, *Nunc Dimittis* at Evensong. *Te Deum Laudamus* becomes easy to use when its structure is made

[29] In 1549 the canticle *Benedicite Omnia Opera* was ordered to be used instead during Lent, but now it is a permissible alternative at any season. In 1552 Ps. 100 was provided as an alternative to *Benedictus* when this hymn occurred in the Lessons: similar alternatives, presumably for the same reason, were provided for the two canticles at Evensong.

clear. The 1928 Prayer Book has done useful service in printing it so as to show at a glance the four sections into which this hymn falls (a) The praise of God by all Creation, ending with the *Sanctus*. (b) The praise of God by the Church (Apostles, Prophets, Martyrs) ending in the Confession of faith in the Trinity. (c) The praise of the incarnate and glorified Christ, ending with a prayer that we may be numbered with His Saints. (d) A short series of Versicles and Responses. *Benedictus*, the song of Zacharias, sees Christ's coming as it affects man, bringing to us salvation, mercy, deliverance, forgiveness, light and guidance. It brings the promises of God home to us individually and so prepares the way for the reciting of the Creed which was used at our own Baptism.

In *Magnificat* we join with our Lady in giving thanks for Christ's Incarnation. This song was first sung at the very watershed of all history, when the Old Covenant gave way to the New. How all creation must, humanly speaking, have held its breath in between Gabriel's announcement and Blessed Mary's 'Be it unto me according to thy word'! *Magnificat* celebrates the triumph of this moment and is thus for ever the morning song of our redemption. *Nunc Dimittis*, the song of Simeon, like *Benedictus*, brings the Gospel home to the individual. It leads thus fittingly to the recital of the Apostles' Creed which, as at Mattins, serves as a memorial of Baptism in which each of us was initiated into the privileges and responsibilities of the Church. The sign of the cross, often made when reciting this creed, is reminiscent also of the solemn signing at Baptism. (On certain days *Quicunque vult*, the Athanasian Creed, is ordered to be said in the place of the Apostles' Creed at Mattins. But its use is now too infrequent to make comment here of much use. Being both precise in its statements and uncompromising in its temper, it has become irretrievably unpopular.)

We now arrive at the climax of the whole office—the recitation of the Lord's Prayer. Some clergymen, irritated by the occurrence of this prayer at two moments in the service, and desiring to reduce these to one, take it upon themselves to leave out 'Our Father' at this point. In this they greatly err, for the whole Office leads up, as it were, to the Lord's Prayer. When in the late seventeenth century Cardinal Tommasi wished to compile an Office Book which would represent a return to liturgical antiquity and from which later and less useful accretions had been pruned, his Offices all found their climax in *Our Father* without the addition of even a solitary Collect in support. So greatly did that learned man appreciate the importance of the Lord's Prayer as the climax of Christian worship. If the twofold appearance of *Paternoster* in Mattins or Evensong be resented, it is the use of this prayer in the introductory part of the service which should be discontinued, as permitted in the 1928 Prayer Book, and not on any account its principal use after the Apostles' Creed.

But the compilers of the Prayer Book were not as austere as Cardinal Tommasi, and in its services the Lord's Prayer is 'supported', both morning and evening, by three Collects. These Collects are introduced by a number of Versicles and Responses. This is a form of liturgical prayer which is always popular, a form which has been described as 'a fervent dialogue between priest and people'. For 'there is nothing more natural to man than "back-chat"; and this remains true even when the back-chat is ecclesiastically termed Versicles and Responses'.[30] The Collect for the day, followed by the two fixed Collects, brings the main part of the service to a close. After the Anthem, or more usually in parish churches, a hymn (from an unofficial hymn book) comes a final group of prayers. These are often referred to as the State Prayers owing to their inclusion of prayers for the Queen, Royal Family and Parliament. Yet in spite of this it is, very commonly, these very prayers which are omitted from the group. As has been already noted, there is a strange reluctance to pray for the Sovereign and all constituted authority at public worship, all the stranger in days when the Queen and the Royal Family have never been so popular. This is all the more regrettable at a time when the whole notion of government is being

[30] *The London Adventure*, Arthur Machen (Martin Secker, 1924), p. 104.

degraded throughout the world, and when the possession of coercive power is coming to be regarded as the only true title to authority. What better witness to the truth can be given by a Christian community than the regular use of a prayer beginning:

> O Lord our heavenly Father, high and mighty, King of kings, Lord of lords, the only Ruler of princes, who dost from thy throne behold all the dwellers upon earth . . . ?

The prayer for Parliament is likewise a glorious supplication, rooted in Biblical conceptions of divine justice and providence and couched in language both simple and dignified; but how often do we hear it? Seldom has it been more necessary than to-day for intercession to be made 'for kings and all that are in high place',[31] and there must be few more suitable instruments for such intercession than the prayers provided for use at Mattins and Evensong in the Book of Common Prayer.

Indeed the whole character of this concluding section has undergone a great transformation in recent years and it is commonly regarded as a part of the service which may be wholly improvised by the presiding minister. In some places the result may have some merit, but in others there is a descent into the banal and sentimental which is quite abominable. Some freedom to improvise is probably desirable, but not to the extent of 'swamping' the prayers provided in the Book, which should always dominate this concluding portion of the Office.

The sermon which usually follows the service and the hymns with which it is often too lavishly interlarded are outside the scope of this book.

Such great liberties are taken with the ordering of both these services in all too many churches that their true character is badly obscured. It is not easy to see how such wanton handling can be reconciled with the promise at Ordination

[31] I Tim. 2.2.

(and at Institution to a benefice) to use the Book of Common Prayer at church services. But signs are not wanting of a return to better things, and who knows whether the merits and virtues of the 1662 Prayer Book may not once more come into their own after the long flirtation with less estimable and less suitable ideals of worship. It cannot, however, be too heavily emphasized that such a return must be accompanied with patient and regular instruction upon the ethos and history of the Prayer Book services and of their practical use as a means of personal and congregational devotion.

Above all, a regular and disciplined life, with its times of prayer and Bible reading, must be held up as a necessity if attendance at public worship is to be more than a mere formality. Public worship is more difficult than solitary worship, and it can only be learned by one who is faithful in the latter. It must be almost impossible to teach people how to use the psalms in church if they don't read the Bible or say their prayers at home.

## X

## PRAYER BOOK REVISION

THE second half of this book has been mainly occupied with a consideration of the Book of Common Prayer in the version issued in the year 1662. The plan has been to indicate how the orders for Mattins and Evensong and the Holy Communion can serve the devotional needs of Anglican congregations. But since 1953, when this book was first published, the movement for revising the 1662 Prayer Book has gained such momentum that it seems useful to devote a final chapter to discussing both the need for revision and the type of services which may emerge from the process.

People often ask why Prayer Book revision is necessary. In a world where so much is rapidly changing, often for the worse, can we not keep our hands off the Church Service which we have known all our lives and which has entered so intimately and powerfully into our whole national history? To this it must be replied that, whether we like it or not, revision is actually going on, though mostly in unauthorized and individual ways. And it is not only the clergy who are to blame for changing services. Hardly a baptism or a funeral or a wedding takes place without some petition from the laity for an omission here or an addition there, each of which means a departure, however modest, from the Prayer Book order. Few individuals indeed desire much change. But the desires of each differ, so that when the total amount of change thought necessary is added up the result would be revolution! When people say they want almost no changes in the Prayer Book they really mean that they want their own wishes to be honoured but not those of other people!

Next it will be said that an attempt has already been made to revise the Prayer Book.[1] In 1928, after many years hard work, was issued 'The Book of Common Prayer with the additions and deviations proposed in 1928'. This volume is commonly referred to as the *Revised Prayer Book*, or more briefly the *1928 Book*. Though not frequently provided for use by the congregation in its complete form, it is nevertheless to be found in the Vicar's stall in the chancel, or on the altar desk of probably a large majority of churches. A great deal of its material is widely used, and in particular much advantage is taken of the rubrics permitting alteration or modification of directions given in the official Prayer Book. But still the main hope of those who most ardently supported the 1928 Book has not been realized. This, of course, was that the acceptance and use of the additions and deviations of the revised book would bring to an end the excessive variety of forms of worship in the Church of England and would produce a liturgical unity (with authoritative diversity) of which we were and still are in great need. The 1928 Book itself almost added to liturgical confusion by providing so many alternatives. It is at best a means for 'patching up' and a provision of 'first aid' to those who find the Prayer Book difficult to use with scrupulous fidelity. Its crowning achievement, the revised Eucharist, though welcomed by a few, has failed to commend itself to the Church as a whole. Liturgical scholarship, almost everywhere, would now consider the service an anachronism. These are some of the reasons why the additions and deviations put forward in 1928 will not by themselves suffice the contemporary demand for revision, even though quite a lot of its material may in one way or another be incorporated in future proposals for change. Next it must be remembered that the Church of England does not stand alone. Along with the Episcopal Church in Scotland, we are the parent unit of a great family of provinces and dioceses scattered throughout the world and known as the Anglican Communion.

[1] Whenever the title 'the Prayer Book' is used in this chapter it will mean the book published in 1662, and now provided for use in the majority of churches.

Our relations with this mighty federation of Churches are close and intimate, and more than just the possession of historical links with one another. Within the component Churches of the Anglican Communion desire for the revision of service books has long been effective. The Protestant Episcopal Church in the United States of America has for some years had its Standing Liturgical Commission which is gradually reviewing its official Prayer Book and is amassing a growing number of 'Prayer Book Studies' which will greatly facilitate the work of actual revision as soon as this is begun. The Anglican Church of Canada at its General Synod of 1959 adopted a completely new revision of the Book of Common Prayer for permissive use. The Church of India, Pakistan, Burma and Ceylon has its new Prayer Book ready for formal authorization. The small and struggling Church of Japan has revised its Eucharistic rite. Even the Church of England in Australia and Tasmania, for long suspicious of Prayer Book Revision, is becoming more than interested. All this at least hints that the urge to compile new forms of public worship is no mere local or passing fashion. Nor is it only Anglican Churches who are active in this movement. For some years now what is called the Liturgical Movement has been at work in the Roman Catholic Church, both in Europe and beyond, a movement which seeks primarily to restore to the laity its place in public worship which had become lost in the Middle Ages. This movement has been responsible, directly or indirectly, for a number of changes in Roman Catholic services. The 'dialogue mass' has been introduced; the Holy Week services have been made more intelligible to the people; larger parts of the services may be celebrated in the mother-tongue instead of in Latin; the Eucharist may be offered in the evening and Holy Communion given within the Eucharist—and so on. Among the Evangelical churches on the Continent there is a revived interest in the problems and art of public worship, especially among Scandinavian and German Lutherans and among Swiss Calvinists. From all of which it will be deduced that new methods of worship are demanded by the inherent situation of the day in which the Church finds itself. There is an inner compulsion which drives Christians on to find more suitable and appropriate ways of worship, to match the opportunities and conflicts of the hour. Speaking of this widespread movement among Christian bodies, the Lambeth Conference Prayer Book Committee said: 'And because this Liturgical Movement has already begun to draw Christians closer to one another in thought and ways of worship, we cannot wish that our own Communion should stand aside.'

These, then, are some of the reasons for being interested in Prayer Book revision, however distasteful the prospect may seem.

*The Process of Revision*

By what sort of method is it hoped to induce the parishes of the Church of England to accept new forms of service? In 1927 the plan was to issue a complete book containing the new services which, had they secured the consent of Parliament, would have come immediately into use. This would have meant that much of the new material would have come as a complete surprise to the great majority of church people. People don't like surprises in church and are apt to feel antagonized from the beginning.

The plan devised for the future revision aims not at suddenly confronting people with a completely new Prayer Book, but at revising services one by one, and not finally authorizing them for use until each has been experimentally used for a period of years. Legislation is being prepared by Convocation which if passed will enable such a process to become recognized by law. In this way new forms of worship will be thoroughly tested as to their value and usefulness before they become the official forms of Church of England worship. In the process of experimental use many of the originally proposed services will no doubt be modified and in some instances considerably altered. A great many of the defects of the 1928 Book might have been avoided if the services had been actually tried out in parish churches up and down the country instead of being presented to the Church as a *fait accompli*. It is true, of course, that some confusion may result from this process, but then confusion is already a condition with which we are familiar. The confusion which results from authorized experimental use will at any rate contain within itself the seeds of hope! The only alternative would be to resort once again to the Tudor and Stuart method of producing a complete Prayer Book and ordering its use. It is certain that such a course would not today be tolerated, either by the clergy or the laity.

*Principles of Revision*

Can anything be said as to what elements of the Prayer Book, as we now have it, are likely to disappear, or be radically altered, in the impending Revision of the next ten to fifteen years? Or, further, is it too early to predict to what extent present liturgical fashions are likely to develop and to become accepted and authoritative methods of worship throughout the Church of England in the future? These are big questions which cannot be answered in detail, but there are pointers in the contemporary life of the Church which may accurately indicate the way things are moving in the realm of worship.

Of all the Lambeth Conferences held, from the first (in 1867) until the ninth (in 1958) the last session gave the most searching and informed investigation to the Prayer Book and its future. The Prayer Book Committee of this Conference presented a very full report, for which only its thirty-three members were responsible. But the full Conference passed eight resolutions which have behind them the authority of the whole body of bishops assembled. Among these resolutions was 74 (c), which runs: 'The Conference . . . urges that a chief aim of Prayer Book Revision should be to further that recovery of the worship of the Primitive Church which was the aim of the compilers of the first Prayer Books of the Church of England.'

This resolution lays down a principle of the most far-reaching importance in the work of revision. When Cranmer and his associates sat down to re-cast the forms of worship of the Church of England, it was their aim to go behind the forms which had come down through the Middle Ages and to try to recover the earlier types of liturgical prayer characteristic of Christian antiquity. It was thought that in this way a purer form of worship would emerge and that the limitations and misdirections of late medieval services would be avoided. If it were asked what precise period of Christian antiquity Cranmer had in mind as his source for revised forms of worship, it would not be easy to give an exact answer. But when he spoke of 'the Primitive Church' or of 'the godly and decent order of the ancient Fathers' he seems to have been speaking in a quite elastic way of pre-medieval times: of the days which were nearer the apostolic age and long previous to the growth of the Papacy as an administrative power: of the centuries in which Church services were conducted in the mother-tongue and were intensely congregational: when public worship was full of substantial readings from the Scriptures and of regular and frequent exposition of the Bible in sermons: of the times previous to the doctrine of Transubstantiation, before interest in the Real Presence came to dominate the Eucharist and when some remembrance of what sacrifice really meant still existed. Other things might be said of this epoch, as that it was previous to the Great Schism between East and West, and also contained centuries during which the Church was still a minority in a pagan world, though these might not have been of special interest to Cranmer and other Reformers who spoke with approval of the Primitive Church.

By the standards of the worship of this period, then, it was to be decided what could most fittingly be used in the sixteenth-century Church of England. Yet though Cranmer rightly divined the ethos of worship in the Primitive Church, he did not, and indeed could not, possess sufficient knowledge of the actual liturgical texts used at that time, or even of the broad outlines of service as given in documents which have become available since his time. It is doubtful if even the liturgical passages in Justin Martyr's *Apologies* were accessible to him, while other sources such as the *Didache*, the *Pilgrimage of Etheria*, Bishop Serapion's *Sacramentary*, and the *Apostolic*

*Tradition of Hippolytus* were not discovered before the last decade of the nineteenth century.

Cranmer's attempt at recovery of the worship of the Primitive Church suffered not only from want of documentary evidence but also from a belief that certain liturgical tendencies of his day were primitive when in fact they were late medieval in origin. Characteristic of this was the great emphasis given to the narrative of the institution in the Eucharistic prayer of consecration and of setting the whole Eucharistic action against a dominant background of Calvary: the enlargement of the penitential element was another instance and more could be quoted.

Yet in spite of this confusion and in spite of the impossibility of knowing much about Primitive Church liturgy at that time, Cranmer was wonderfully successful in producing forms of service which were in most ways a great improvement upon late medieval worship and which became on the whole extremely popular within the Church of England, and in later times an object of some envy among members of other Christian bodies. For the restored use of the mother tongue and of the active and vocal part given to the laity in the liturgy, the recovery of Biblical lections and of frequent preaching became as popular features of public worship as they were authentic elements of pre-medieval use.

Yet it is significant that, when in our own day Christians of various denominations came to form themselves into a united body called the Church of South India, they did not base their new forms upon those of the Book of Common Prayer nor upon those of any other book of worship reformed since the sixteenth century. Instead they had recourse to that new knowledge of how the Primitive Church prayed which has become available in modern times. The result is a liturgy which a French Roman Catholic scholar has described as 'more Catholic than the English Book of Common Prayer'. In the same spirit the Prayer Book Committee of the 1958 Lambeth Conference said: 'We might ask what elements in the Book of Common Prayer are due to the sixteenth- and seventeenth-century misunderstanding of what is "primitive" in public worship, and what elements need to be substituted or added in order to make Prayer Book services truer to the ideal towards which Cranmer was feeling his way.'[2]

In January 1960 new forms of Baptism and Confirmation came before the Convocations of Canterbury and York. The compilers of these forms had deliberately avoided taking Cranmer's services as their model (as the revisers of the 1928 Book had done). Instead they based their forms upon what the scholarship of the last fifty years has revealed as characteristic of the Initiatory rites of pre-medieval Christian antiquity. In the Convocation of Canterbury two speakers, each of considerable influence in their different schools of thoughts, commended the line taken by the compilers of these services. They said that agreement in the Church on new sacramental services was unlikely unless an attempt was made, not to patch up and improve upon Cranmer's services, but to go right behind the controversies of the Reformation and the Middle Ages. This, as has been pointed out, was the recommendation of the latest Lambeth Conference.

*Practical Implications*

All this may sound rather vague, and it may be asked whether it is possible to give detailed illustrations of how the adoption of this principle would work out in practice.

The Lambeth Conference commended to the study of the whole Anglican Communion the counsel on Prayer Book Revision given in the report of the sub-committee. Part of this was a section entitled ' Suggested modifications or additions for the further recovery of other elements of the worship of the Primitive Church'. The section is quoted in order to illustrate the practical implications of the principle:

' 1. Exhortations have a legitimate function in the liturgy, but they should be shorter and fewer.

[2] *The Lambeth Conference 1958*, p. 2.80.

'2. The present corporate expressions of penitence need to be modified both in length and language.

'3. More extensive provision of litanies, with shorter clauses, for corporate intercession, thanksgiving, and adoration; with the discouragement of long strings of collects or other prayers for this purpose.

'4. The recovery of the "People's Prayers" at the Eucharist by breaking up the Prayer for the Church into sections, each followed by congregational response, or into a litany with short clauses.

'5. The Offertory, with which the people should be definitely associated, to be more closely connected with the Prayer of Consecration.

'6. The events for which thanksgiving is made in the Consecration Prayer are not to be confined to Calvary but include thanksgiving for all the principal "mighty works of God", especially the resurrection and the ascension of our Lord and his return in glory.'[3]

Suggestions of a more or less detailed kind were also made upon the first part of the Communion service, commonly called the Ante-Communion, when celebrated on Sundays. The insertion of a lesson from the Old Testament between the Collect and the Epistle was suggested, while the three lessons could be separated by psalms or by portions of psalms. This was proposed in view of the extensive growth of the Sunday 'Parish Communion' which usually displaces Mattins. By adding psalms and an Old Testament Lesson to the Ante-Communion some of the values of Mattins could be preserved in the Eucharist.

Suggestions were also made for the revision of Baptism and Confirmation, and some of the more important points have been incorporated in the proposals made by the Liturgical Commission of the Church of England referred to above.

[3] *The Lambeth Conference 1958*, p. 2.81.

It is not probable that the offices of Mattins and Evensong will need much revision. They already breathe so much of the atmosphere of the Primitive Church. Though there are from time to time complaints about the amount of psalmody which has to be sung, they are very popular forms of devotion still. Considerable improvement to Mattins would result if *Benedictus* changed places with *Te Deum*. *Benedictus* at Mattins corresponds in function to *Magnificat* at Evensong. It belongs to the threshold leading from the Old to the New Covenant and is most effective when used in this position. On the other hand, *Te Deum* is so completely a confession of Christian doctrine that a place immediately following the New Testament Lesson is highly appropriate.

Two of the chief needs of our services are the revision of the Collects, Epistles, and Gospels appointed for Sundays and Holy Days, and the provision of a much fuller series for use on Black Letter saints' days and for ordinary weekdays than was afforded by the 1928 Book. Some of the Sunday Epistles are notoriously difficult to understand and there is an apparent lack of cohesion between the Epistles and Gospels which could be adjusted. Further, if an Old Testament lesson is to be introduced for use at the Sunday Eucharist, a good deal of re-arrangement would be desirable if some sort of compatibility between the teaching of the three lections is to be achieved. New Sunday collects might with advantage be provided on some occasions. The present collect for Passion Sunday, for instance, might well give place to something more obviously suitable to that particular day. Not much has been done so far in this particular field, though suggestions for Eucharistic psalms and Old Testament lessons have been made in the Canadian and Indian prayer books.

As for Black Letter days, most people find that the 1928 series is not full enough. It provides an admirable series of Epistles and Gospels for every weekday in Lent and in Easter week, but those put out for actual saints' days are not always satisfactory and there are too few alternatives. A generous provision of alternative sets of collects, epistles, and gospels to be available for use on the different classes of saints' days is urgently needed. It is for lack of such provision that churches with a daily Eucharist often forsake the Prayer Book and take up with some unauthorized altar book of dubious quality. The habit thus begun is apt to stay and its principle (or lack of principle) comes to be applied throughout the services to the detriment of a sound liturgical life in the parish.

But even when there are no Black Letter feasts with their special observance, weekdays could well be provided with their own epistles and gospels. The old Salisbury missal used to put out special lessons for the Wednesdays and Fridays of Advent, and for the Wednesdays in the weeks after Pentecost, thus providing plenty of variety for weekday celebrations. A similar plan might with great advantage be adopted by a new Prayer Book.

*Conclusion*

Such, then, is the path which Prayer Book revision may follow, though it is not claimed here to give a detailed forecast. Very little, it will be noticed, has been said about the future Prayer of Consecration in the Eucharist, partly because the Lambeth Conference dealt with it in such general terms and did not aspire to pronounce in detail upon it. But it is unlikely that agreement could be reached merely by touching up and amending our existing use.

Much has been said here about the Primitive Church. But it must not be thought that the present interest in the worship of that age is due to a desire to idolize the past and to reproduce its services in the worship of the Church to-day. There is a suspicion in some quarters that to speak of the Primitive Church is to betray a desire to 'put the clock back'. Yet, as Mr C. S. Lewis once said, there are occasions when 'putting the clock back' is a necessity if we are truly to advance. If the clock is fast you must put it back in order to know where you are. There are times when, if you have taken a wrong turning, you must go back in order to find again the road which you missed but which will lead you to the place you really want to reach. There can be little doubt that in the Middle Ages the Church did take wrong turnings in the field of public worship. The Middle Ages ended in the break-up of Christendom into a number of separate bodies. To some extent methods of worship must have been responsible for this tragedy. It seems, therefore, the wisest task to return to the study of pre-medieval worship, not in order to imitate, but in order to receive guidance. Taught by the experience of those ages we shall be the better able to advance and to find forms of worship which will draw Christians together instead of forcing them apart. Now that we at last know so much more about earlier worship than has been the case for many hundreds of years, we cannot throw away that knowledge without learning from it and extracting principles which will be of the greatest practical use.

All the same, the time before us is not going to be easy. Revision of forms of worship is a slow and difficult process. The Church of England Liturgical Commission took over three years very hard work in order to produce its proposals for Baptism and Confirmation. But the publication of its suggested rites is not the end. The services are not even now available for experimental use. That will not be until the necessary legislation is passed. When it is passed, a period of up to seven years will be necessary for experimental use of the services before they can again come before the Convocations. Criticisms will then have to be made and met and slowly some agreed form will have to emerge. Nor are Baptism and Confirmation the only services which will have to go through this mill. There is the Eucharist itself and all the other rites of the Church contained in the Book of Common Prayer.

All this will mean for the parishes of our land a longish time of apparent instability and uncertainty, a time even of increased confusion in some ways.

Above all things there will be the danger lest perpetual experiment may have an unsettling effect: the notion of liturgy as something authoritatively 'given' for our use may, if we are not careful, grow weaker. The Church of England must resolutely hold before itself the aim of once more establishing among us the concept of what used to be called 'the Church Service'. In the piecemeal revision, which seems quite necessary in the present situation, we may find ourselves losing the sense of the Liturgy as a unity and seeing not the wood but the trees. It is to be hoped that realizing this danger we shall be helped resolutely to keep before our eyes the one-ness of the Church's worship and its necessary authority as expressing the mind of the Church.

# GENERAL INDEX

Abo, 63
Absolution, 95
Adoration, 26, 53
Advent Sunday, 73, 74
*Agnus Dei*, 45
Agricola, Michael, 63
Alexander, Abp. Wm., 51
Altar, 52, 79, 81, 84f., 93, 94
Ante-Communion, 67, 94, 133
Anthem, 45, 122
Articles, The Thirty-Nine, 57, 110
Ascension, 24, 79
Athanasius, St., 107 Creed of, 121
Atomic bomb, 35
Augustine, St., 36, 110n.
Authority, 39, 56, 57, 68

Baptism, 15, 52, 54, 85f.
Baptism and Confirmation, 132, 136
Basil, St., 41
Bell, Dr. G. K. A., 56
*Benedicite*, 73, 120n.
*Benedictus*, 73, 120, 121, 134
Benson, Fr. R. M., 19, 111
Berry, C. Leo, 96, 99
Bible, 33, 39, 50, 62, 65, 66, 70, 71, 72
Bidding of the Bedes, 62
Blood, 80, 81
Body and Blood of Christ, 97-99
Body of Christ, 15, 86, 99
*Burial of the Dead*, 105
Burkitt, Prof. E. C., 99, 106
Bussard, Fr. P., 63

Calendar, 74, 90
Calvary, 85, 88
Candles, 54, 57
Canon (of the Eucharist), 96-97
Canticles, 103, 119

Catechism, the Prayer Book, 98
Cathedral, 42, 45-47
Ceremonial, 50-60, 61-62; foreign, 59; and Romanticism, 56
Ceremonies, Of (Preface), 58
Chancel, 94
Chanting, 42, 43, 44
Charles II, King, 68
Choirs, Cathedral, 47; Parochial, 45, 49
Christ, as Mediator of worship, 15, 16, 27; as offerer of perfect worship, 21-23; Passion of, 22
Christmas, 74, 101
Church, 91, 112, 113, 114, 121
Church militant (Prayer for), 89, 92, 94
Climate of opinion, 37-39
Collection (at Offertory), 93
Collects, 33, 73, 75, 90, 91, 101
Comfortable words, 95
Common Prayer, *see* Prayer Book
Communion, *see* Holy Communion
Communion, annual, 66-67
Communion of Priest and People, 96-97
Confession, 53, 95, 104
Consecration, prayer of, 96, 97, 99
Cranmer, Abp. Thos., 59, 67, 68, 101, 129-132
Creed, Apostles', 74, 121; Athanasian, 121; Nicene, 42, 91
Cross, the, 22, 85, 86, 97; sign of, 52, 91
Cyril, St., 64

Davidson, Abp. Randall, 56, 103, 118
Davison, W. T., 110n.
Death, 79, 81, 84f.
*Didache*, 130
Dix, Dr. Gregory, 23n.
Doxology, 100
Draw near, 94-95

# INDEX

Easter, 63, 101
Ecstasy, 42, 43, 44
Edification, 65, 67, 92
*Eikon Basilike*, 37
Eliot, George, 33
Elizabeth I, Queen, 68
English (language), 64, 65
Epistle (liturgical), 43, 75, 90, 91, 134
Erastianism, 90
Eternity, worship a preparation for, 17-18
Eucharist, 45, 53, 54, 62, 67, 75, 78, 80, 86, 87, 88, 89ff., 103
Evensong, 46, 48, 66, 70, 71, 73, 75, 102ff.
Exhortations, 65, 69, 89

Farm Sunday, 11
Festivals, 60, 66, 70, 75
Finland, 63
Focus of devotion, 53
Free Churches, 58, 103
Freemasonry, 60

Gethsemane, 23, 95, 113
*Gloria in excelsis*, 42, 101
*Gloria Patri*, 105, 106
Gore, Bp. Charles, 90
Gospel (liturgical), 43, 75, 90, 91, 134
Goudge, Dr. H. L., 116
Greek (language), 64

Heaven and worship, 10, 17, 35, 55; and sacrifice, 85, 86, 94, 96
Hebert, Fr. A. G., 97
Hebrews, Epistle to the, 83f., 95, 98n.
Hicks, Bp. F. C. N., 79
*Hippolytus*, The Apostolic Tradition of, 131
Hislop, D. H., 29
Hodgson, Prof. L., 105n.
Holy Communion, 16, 62, 66, 67, 75, 77
Holy Spirit, 16, 27, 31, 32, 33
Hooker, Richard, 41
Hoskyns, Sir E., 29, 31

Humble Access, prayer of, 95-96
Hymns, 103, 109, 122, 123

Imprecatory Psalms, 115-117
Incarnation, 31
Incense, 53, 57
Industrial Sunday, 11
Inflexions, 43, 44
Intention (Eucharistic), 92
Interpolations into Liturgy, 40

James I, King, 68
Justin Martyr, 34

King, Bp. Edward, 54
*Kyrie Eleison*, 90, 101

Laity, House of, 118
Lambeth Conference, 128, 129, 131, 132
Last Supper, 23, 78, 93, 97
Latin (language), 61, 64
Lessons (Bible), 73, 74, 92, 119, 120, 133, 134
Lewis, C. S., 38
Litany, the English, 64, 66, 67, 75
Liturgical Movement, The, 127
Liturgical Year, 73, 75
Liturgy, 17, 35, 36, 39, 72, 75; language of, 64; revision of, 37
Lord's Prayer, 34, 43, 89, 96, 98, 121, 122
Love, 19-20, 26

*Magnificat*, 49, 120, 121, 134
Mass, 62, 64, 65, 77, 88
Mattins, 66, 67, 70, 71, 73, 75, 102ff.
Memorial (sacrificial), 97
Memory, a perpetual, 97
Middle Ages, 56, 61, 66, 72, 88, 102
*Missa Catechumenorum*, 89, 92
*Missa Fidelium*, 89

# INDEX

Music, congregational, 45; choral, 45; reasons for in worship, 41-42; unison, 49

NEWMAN, Dr. J. H., 20
Nicodemus, 30
Noah, 78, 79
Nonconformist, 68
*Nunc Dimittis*, 120, 121

OBEDIENCE, 85, 86
Oblation, prayer of, 96, 98, 100, 100n., 101
Offertory, 53, 54, 92, 93, 94
Office, the Divine, 66, 102
Olaus Petri, 63
Omissions (of parts of liturgy), 40
Ornaments Rubric, 59
Orthodox Church, 89
Oxford Movement, 56

PAUL, St., 36, 78
Piano, 36
Plainsong, 48-49
Pleading (Christ's sacrifice), 80, 86
Poetry, 44, 103
Prayer, of Christ, 25; *extempore*, 33-35; pre-meditated, 34; with the understanding, 32, 34
Prayer Book, The, 39, 40, 57, 59, 61, 62, 64, 65, 68, 69, 70, 73; of 1549, 52n., 59n., 61, 67; of 1552, 68, 89; of 1662, 89, 96, 124; of 1928, 71, 73, 89n., 96, 99, 104, 121
Preaching, 62, 65
*Preces*, 105
Preparation, at Holy Communion, 89; at Mattins and Evensong, 104
Primer, 62
Primitive Church, The, 130, 131, 134
Prodigal son, 53
Proper Preface, 75
Protestant, 67, 68
Public Worship, attempts to defend, 9-10; attentiveness at, 39-40, 104; definition of, 31; and Heaven, 10, 17; low opinion of, 7-9; regarded as propaganda, 11, 12, 39
Pullan, Dr. Leighton, 63

QUAKERS, 30, 51, 52
Queen, collect for the, 90; prayers for the, 122
Quick, Dr. O. C., 83
*Quicunque vult*, 121
Quignon, *see* Quinonez
Quinonez, Cardinal, 63, 66

RATCLIFF, Prof. E. C., 102
Redemption, memorial of, 73, 74, 103, 104
Reformation, 57, 58, 63, 65, 67
Reformers, continental, 67
Regalism, 90
Remembrance (of Christ), 97
Remembrance Day, 11
Resurrection, 24, 85, 86, 112
Revelation of St. John, 24, 79
Roche, Fr. W., 38n.
Roman Catholics, 77, 102, 106
Rubrics, 56, 59, 75, 120

SACRAMENT, the Holy, 52, 62
Sacrifice, 51, 52, 68, 78ff., 88ff.; 'of praise and thanksgiving', 98f.
*Sanctus*, 42
Scott, Sir Walter, 56
Scott-Holland, Canon H., 54
Scripture, Holy, *see* Bible
Sermon, 12, 65, 91, 92; *see* Preaching
Sermon on the Mount, 9, 79
Shaw, Bernard, 78
Shaw, Dr. Geoffrey, 101n.
'Shortened' services, 13, 103
Sin, 85, 100; definition of, 20; and Christ's Passion, 22
Slavonic (language), 64
'Solemn' Eucharist, 92
'Special Services', 11, 12, 69
Spiritual, 29-31
Srawley, Dr. J. H., 93n.
Stanley, Dean A. P., 56
State Prayers, 122-123
Summary of the Law, 90
Superstition, 63
*Sursum Corda*, 96
Sweden, 63

## INDEX

TABLE, the Holy, 93, 94
Taylor, Jeremy, 33
*Te Deum Laudamus*, 73, 120, 134
Temple, Abp. Wm., 51
Ten Commandments, 90
Thanksgiving, prayer of, 96*n*., 100, 100*n*.
Tommasi, Cardinal, 122
Tractarians, 56
Tradition, 55, 56, 59
Transfiguration, 23, 84
Trent, Council of, 64
Trinity, the Blessed, 26, 76

UNDERHILL, Miss E., 68
Unison (singing), 49
Unitarian, 33

*Venite exultemus Domino*, 105, 119
Versicles and Responses, 105, 122
Victim, 79ff., 83f., 93, 100
Vine, 15, 113, 114
Voice, the natural, 43

WESTCOTT, Dr. B. F., 31
Wied, Hermann von, 63
Wordsworth, Bp. John, 66
Worship, acceptable, 16; definition of, 14, 19, 26, 27, 52; the end of, 28; as exercise, 36-37; value of fixed forms, 34-39, 74; mediated by Christ, 15-16; instinct for, 16; issues in obedience, 19; perversion of instinct, 14; why public, 14-15, 29; spiritual, 29-31

www.ingramcontent.com/pod-product-compliance
Lightning Source LLC
Chambersburg PA
CBHW072154160426
43197CB00012B/2378